CAR DESIGN ASIA

Paolo Tumminelli

MYTHS, BRANDS, PEOPLE

teNeues

- **4 START**
- **7 EAST ASIA**
- **19 TRANSISTOR**
  PRINCE 29; HINO 33; KEI CAR 38; HIDEYUKI MIYAKAWA 42.
- **51 JAP AM**
  DATSUN 61; TOYOTA 65; EIJI TOYODA 66; MITSUBISHI 85.
- **95 IKONIK**
  YAMAHA 111; ISUZU 113; SHINICHIRO SAKURAI 115; YUTAKA KATAYAMA 116; SOICHIRO HONDA 121; WASABI KEI 123; TSUNEJI MATSUDA 129.
- **135 FULL FLAT**
  BOSOZOKU 156; VANS 162; HONDA 165; LAND CRUISER 168.

173 ANIMOTION
ACURA 188; **ABC ROADSTER** 190; **CUTE CAR** 192;
PAIKUKA 195; **EUNOS** 196; **EFINI** 198; **MAZDA** 199; **SUZUKI** 202;
SUBARU 204; **DAEWOO** 205.

215 HY BREED
LEXUS 234; **TALL BOY** 238; **SCION** 241;
WiLL 242; **MITSUOKA** 243; **DAIHATSU** 244; **SSANGYONG** 245;
HYBRID SHAPE 249; **CROSSOVER** 254; **NISSAN** 256.

265 DRIVE OUT
KIA 274; **HYUNDAI** 280; **INFINITI** 286;
EQUUS 290; **QOROS** 297.

300 REGISTER

START

If a motto were needed for *Car Design Asia*, then "the last ones shall be first" would be a perfect fit. Back in 2010, I started working on a car design trilogy: Europe, America, and—obviously—Japan. Living in Europe, such was our interest in novelty and the undiscovered that the publisher and I agreed to begin with the last. The 3/11 earthquake forced us to change plans, for it simply did not seem appropriate to bother a country deeply affected by such tragic circumstances with enquiries about old cars. But three years later, having completed both *Car Design Europe* and *Car Design America*, the automotive landscape in East Asia had changed substantially. Not only had the leading manufacturers from South Korea—Hyundai and Kia—fully emancipated themselves into global design players, but even China—emerging since 2009 as the world's largest producer of, as well as the largest market for cars—had started declaring its independence from the Western design world. In return, the leading exporters to China, among them all the German premium manufacturers, had obviously begun adapting their design strategies to the needs, wishes, and dreams of their newest and largest clientele. The Japanese reaction to this creative insurgence was quick—even by Japanese standards. All of a sudden, the whole automotive world was transformed. With East Asia now at the focus, the title of this book was accordingly changed from *Japan* to *Asia*. This certainly does not deprive the Japanese automotive industry of its leading position among East Asian competitors, which is not only due to its more substantial history, but also because of its status as a role model for global business. Yet no matter how impressive the numbers may be, as automobile design is a cultural phenomenon, its quality is to be judged aside from quantity.

The West's evaluation of Eastern car design has never been particularly polite—primarily, and most easily explicable, because Japan was last to join this line of business. And because she came along slowly and quietly. The Japanese dared doing this in countries where the automobile had and still has to be, first of all, fast and loud as hell. The Western automotive media, and their most fanatical readers, just did not get the tale of the good, reliable Jap car. Luckily, the larger section of the market—people more interested in mobility than cars—did. Starting in 1980, when Japan became the world's leading car manufacturer, this perception began to change rapidly. Again, the last ones became the first. The 1980s were the heyday of the Japanese automobile, crowned with the success of Honda in Formula 1 and embellished with that charming global fetish known to some simply as Eunos Roadster, and as Mazda Miata or MX-5 to others. This, the world's most successful open sports car, was the kind of "machine that changed the world," as celebrated by MIT researchers in their groundbreaking book of 1990. Fifteen years later, Japanese born Ken Okuyama became the first ever *gaijin* director within the holiest of all car design temples: Pininfarina of Turin.

While all this was happening, I realized that nobody knew much about Japanese car design—not even myself. In the days before the internet, the market of the rising sun was almost impenetrable to Western eyes. Even now, cultural differences far beyond simple language barriers render the exploration and interpretation of this sheer, gigantic multitude of rapidly changing models a captivating challenge. While the business history of the Japanese car industry has been the object of a great many substantial publications, design development was not—and certainly not from a cultural standpoint. This is mostly because Japanese companies have seldom been celebrating themselves or their designers, with the consequence that most of them remain unknown to this day. And if the Japanese did not bother to redress that, certainly fewer people abroad would. In a way, I felt someone had to try. Specific literature being scarce, I knocked on several doors in Japan, Europe, and the US, asking experienced professionals to share their recollections and opinions with me. Japanese car design is not univocal, but fragmented into Japanese-Asian, Asian-American and Asian-European influences on brands and models. For the sake of showing the most intimate, less well-known part of the story, I tried my best to select and portray the most Eastern Asian of all designs. Compiling this book thus turned out to be a different exercise in contrast to the previous volumes of my *Car Design* trilogy. Browsing the image archives of all the manufacturers has made me aware of another very peculiar quality. Even for contemporary models, the original lifestyle images I prefer to use in my books are underrepresented, compared to the archives of the more brand-conscious Western manufacturers. The high export rates may surely be responsible for such an obvious abundance of plain still life studio photographs. But what is really striking is how most photo shootings underwent an almost pedantic, very Japanese routine. New models have been shot from the same standard perspectives, following the most precise rules, as far as lighting and camera positioning are concerned—and this across all decades and manufacturers. The result of my findings and considerations is a book that is obviously different from the previous two—yet wonderfully so. Whoever you may consider to be "first" or "last," I am sure you will agree that a book such as this was long due.

Paolo Tumminelli

EAST ASIA

East Asia did not invent the automobile, nor was it particularly fast at developing a car culture of its own. Instead, it made automobility a global issue. One has to wait until 1960 for Japan, 1980 for South Korea and 2000 for China seriously to engage in automobile production. In spite of this late start, by 2012, China ranked first, Japan second, and South Korea fourth among the world's largest manufacturing countries. When dealing with car design from the three largest East Asian manufacturing countries, one big difference needs to be taken note of: while China has been occupied with feeding the hunger of its domestic market, Japan, and later South Korea, had export in mind early on. This is the lesson Japan was taught as early as 1853, when American Commodore Matthew Calbraith Perry's steam-powered ships ripped the curtain that had isolated Tokyo from the rest of the world. Albeit with a delay of almost one century, all of a sudden modernity appeared in mysterious Japan, paving the way towards the enlightened Meiji era. In comparison, China had already enjoyed a long tradition of intense, though ambivalent commercial relationships with the West. In the wake of the Opium Wars, in the mid-1850s, China had lost Hong Kong to Queen Victoria and was forced to grant rights to foreign countries, including establishing diplomatic relationships. On the part of Europe and the United States, a much idealized, pristine Chinese aesthetic had set a persistent trend for *chinoiserie*—furniture, handcraft, fashion, and art inspired by the magical and glamorously baroque style of the Qing, China's last imperial dynasty. It was this fascination exerted by China that inspired a company of European gentlemen to arrange the greatest of all motoring events: the 1907 Peking to Paris race. The recollections of reporter, Luigi Barzini, guest in the winning car of Italian Prince, Scipione Borghese, powerfully highlight the chasm between the East and the West: "The existence of a car in Beijing seemed to me even more absurd than that of a sedan chair over London Bridge." At the start of the race, "on the road, kept free by Chinese soldiers, between two wings of mute people, there remained but the five cars, following

Nanpu bridge, Shanghai, 1991

one another at a speed never ever seen, and possibly never to be seen again within the capital of the Celestial Empire." It actually took 75 years before the first mass production car of Western kind would be seen again in China—the 1982 Volkswagen Santana.

MODERN JAPAN

Japan's approach to modernity was a quicker and more pragmatic one. Mutsushito, the Emperor Meiji, sent delegations to explore the world and hired thousands of foreign experts. The value of such cross-cultural transfer is crucial to understanding Japanese car design, as well. Following Western examples, Japan not only revolutionized its industry, but modernized everything from the military to communications, from public education to banking, and, in 1889, adopted a new, German-inspired constitution. In return, the Western world developed a growing interest in all things Japanese—just like *chinoiserie*, *japonaiserie* became another exotic fad. In order to satisfy mundane curiosity, *Harper's* Magazine sent reporter, Lafcadio Hearn, to Japan in 1890. Influenced by a typically romantic, highly idealized view of Asian aesthetics, he found Tokyo already spoiled by Western habits: that same year, both the Imperial Hotel, designed by German architects, Böckmann & Ende, and Ryōunkaku, a skyscraper designed by Scottish engineer, William Burton, had been inaugurated. No matter how far removed modernity had been from the Japanese intellect, and even though the metallic and the mechanical had never been part of the Japanese design DNA: Japan was eager to learn, finally. In 1901, Locomobile of America started to sell cars in Tokyo, and, as late as 1907, the Takuri Type 3 came out. Not surprisingly, the first Japanese car adopted contemporary European style,

Ryounkaku, Tokyo, 1890

Itala 35/45 HP, Peking, 1907

inspired by Darracq. A mere dozen were made. Japan's first mass produced car, the upper class Mitsubishi model A— designed after a Fiat Tipo 3—arrived ten years later and would not do much better: 22 units between 1917 and '21 were a meager yield indeed. During the same period of time, Ford built short of four million, Buick more than half a million cars—and thousands were sold, even of the big Fiat. The car simply was not a priority in a country with no roads and no places to go to. Instead, Japan was busy reinventing itself as a military world power. The resultant Russo-Japanese War led to the annexation of Korea in 1910—a state of affairs that lasted until 1945 and had a direct effect on the late start of the South Korean automotive industry. It was not just in the aftermath of the First World War, but also due to the tragic consequences of the 1923 earthquake—which had turned Ford trucks into a necessity—that the military-run government was convinced of the strategic importance of the automobile. Initially, the market was left to Ford and, later on, General Motors, against which none of the 16 small and constricted domestic manufacturers could compete. Then, in 1931, the Committee for the Establishment of a Domestic Automobile Industry rapidly drew up plans; in 1936, the Automobile Manufacturing Industries Act was passed, and finally, in 1937, protectionist policies chased Ford and GM out of the market. Out of nowhere, and under precise governmental guidance—similar in spirit to the famed MITI—the Japanese automotive industry was born. But as the manufacturers were still torn between the profitable market for military trucks and the unknown prospects of private mobility, there was neither a real business plan for the Japanese automobile, nor were there any traces of a Japanese car design. Once again, the pragmatic learning-from-abroad approach was chosen. The Nissan Motor Company,

Takuri Type 3, 1907

Mitsubishi Model A, 1917

Toyoda AA, 1936

incorporated in 1934, consequently built a small car, based on the British Austin Seven, and a larger one, based on the American Graham-Paige. Following six years of in-house research, Toyoda Automatic Loom Works began to market its AA model in 1936. Although wholly engineered in Japan, its mechanicals reflected Ford and Chevrolet standards, while its advanced body design appeared like a blueprint of the famed Chrysler Airflow. One year later, the Toyota Motor Corporation was founded—just in time to see Japan entering the second Sino-Japanese War, and then the Second World War.

FIRST DRIVES

It was to a country devastated physically, financially and psychologically by the atomic bomb that Emperor Hirohito gave just the right push: science, and not America, had defeated Japan. Hence capital was directed towards research and development. The knock-down approach seemed to be the quickest way towards reactivating automobile production. In the 1950s, Nissan therefore partnered with Austin, Isuzu with Hillman, Shin-Mitsubishi with Willys-Overland and Hino with Renault—now they were all licensed to assemble models identical or similar to their Western counterparts. Here the old myth of Japanese photocopying of Western design was born. And although engineered and designed in Japan, the Toyota SA of 1947 did vaguely resemble the contemporary Volkswagen. As for the Beetle, the public also gave the lovely car a nickname: Toyopet. With the larger Toyopet Crown of 1955, Japanese design evolved dramatically. Although the style was American-inspired—the Studebaker Champion or 1949 Ford coming to mind— the package of this Japanese 'small car' was definitely unique. Despite their chrome

Isuzu Hillman Minx Super de Luxe, 1959

paraphernalia, which lent them the charms of a "baby Cadillac," cars of this era actually display the sturdiness and performance of a truck. Designed to cope with the horrible conditions of domestic country roads and metropolitan meanders, their bodies were built into narrow vertical proportions. This compactness, mirrored by both the Japanese people and localities, became the very first trademark of Japanese car design. The specific quality of classic Japanese car design—always to borrow something from abroad, while at the same time remaining undeniably unique—was already present, but not yet understood. If the Japanese car lacked anything, than it was the immaterial: the intellectual pathos of the European avant-garde, the dramatic thrill of open-road racing, the excessive richness of the American Way of Life.

This austereness was also what led the manufacturers to agree to feudal constraints regarding matters such as body size, engine displacement, maximum horsepower, or top speed—which was limited to 180 kph for all vehicles for a long time. Japan simply regarded the automobile as a beneficial business. All that was needed to do good business were good cars—not the most beautiful, not the fastest, not the finest. Just good ones. And that certainly was something millions of people around the world could be comfortable, if not happy with!

KING MARKET

To the Japanese, the mass market really was king. They were first worldwide to listen to the teachings of the pioneer of quality management, William Edwards Deming, and those of the father of customer satisfaction practice, J.D. "Dave" Power—both Americans, incidentally. This approach reflects the attitude of a people, educated to think

Toyopet Crown, 1955

and act as members of a community, rather than individuals—and military discipline did the rest. Endless variations of seemingly the same midsize sedan, the family car for the uprising *sararīman*, have been made available in order to satisfy just one single, tiny bit of individual desire, yet without ever denying common sense—or taste. The search for impermanence and uniformity has since been driving the development of Japanese car design. Adding to the disorientation is a design dynamic that is exaggerated even by American standards. One reason for this can be found in the flexibility of the Japanese lean production system. Being experts in miniaturization—think bonsai—in packaging—origami—and in assembling—pagoda—the Japanese understood car manufacturing as a fluid process. They became masters of the assemblage of many smaller parts, quickly and economically produced through the use of smaller moulds. Implementing even the smallest design variations, a nightmare for Western manufacturing systems, was easily accepted as being part of the game. A second reason is due to the complex and interlocking network of retail channels, several for each brand, with each of them featuring a unique range of models and badges. Another reason is a morbid legal maneuver called *shaken*. In Japan, the periodical vehicle inspection compulsory for all cars three years and older, is very strict and gradually becoming extremely expensive. Customers have been educated to rather buy a new car than bear this burden. Driving a newer model—typically of the very same make and type as the previous one—became, if not the source of a little pleasure, then at least a way to contribute to and participate in the welfare state. While rejecting the American policy of the model year change, Toyota and Nissan did generally update their designs every four years, often in more substantial fashion than the Americans

Toyota Corolla, 1966

Toyota Corolla ST, 1975

Toyota Corolla Sprinter SE, 1979

were accustomed to, and twice as fast as most Europeans would do.

MULTIPLICITY

The result of this hyperactive marketing is a nebulous galaxy of names, models, and body styles, which cannot be appreciated from one single market perspective. For the same make and model have rarely been available in all markets under the same name and with the same design features—a highly sophisticated form of badge engineering. As a further consequence, Japanese brands have hardly been able to establish one univocal image. Eyes closed, anybody can recollect the image of a Volkswagen Golf. Yet the same is impossible for the Corolla, despite being, with more than 40 million units sold since 1966, by far the world's most successful car. Each of its ten series shows almost no design continuity; 41 body variations—excluding the Japan-only Sprinter family—add unwanted vagueness, at least by Western criteria. For the Japanese, it must be good this way. Permanence, as embodied by the rock hard, monolithic Western Parthenon, never was highly valued in a country whose very foundations are constantly being shaken by earthquakes. Once again, Donald Richie points out how *fūryū*, the most elegant of styles, is hardly linked to material immortality. Instead, it would be appreciated in the seasonal vanishing of the cherry blossoms or, in a more religious paradigm, in the Shintō shrine of Ise. Since 1241, the precious wooden construction dedicated to the goddess Amaterasu is dismantled every twenty years, only for a new, absolutely identical shrine to be built on a nearby plot—shrine number 63 being due in 2033. There have been as many as ten different models of the monumental Imperial Hotel of 1890 in 90 years, including a much celebrated Frank Lloyd Wright

Toyota Corolla Sprinter Coupé, 1989

Toyota Corolla Compact, 1991

Toyota Corolla Altis, 2013

design from 1920 to '22, which was sadly partially destroyed to make room for a new one. As if to confirm the rule, the car enthusiast can find many notable exceptions across all Japanese makes and models—many of which were designed or at least inspired by the inevitable Italians. Many purely Japanese designs would be called experimental, innovative, or simply exotic if they were of Western origin—one just needs to cast one's mind back to the Nissan EXA, Toyota bB or Subaru Alcyone. Others were utterly evocative, if not provocative: the Eunos Roadster in its masses or the Honda NSX in all its class. Others were of outstanding cleverness, such as the mini-sized *kei* car, this exquisitely small and most uniquely Japanese of all car design concepts. Retrospectively, it seems as though the Japanese were either too shy or too practical to show off with no holds barred. At home, they may have taken some design risks, but abroad they concentrated on adhering to their 'simply good business through simply good cars' formula.

This being said, it comes as no surprise that, by 1980, Japan had become the world's largest manufacturer, attracting both public attention and strong political interference. The appreciation of the yen in 1985 urged the Japanese to reconsider their "good & affordable" positioning and to enter the more profitable premium market with new brands, strategically designed to fight, and therefore initially resembling, the American and European flagship models: Honda's Acura, Nissan's Infiniti, and Toyota's Lexus. The most important consequences of these new political constraints were at an industrial level. One move was to further improve the much celebrated Japanese lean production systems in order to reduce costs to a level previously unheard of. The other move was to open factories abroad, thus bypassing existing export restraints imposed upon Japan. In 1982,

Nissan EXA, 1982

Subaru Alcyone, 1985

Honda NSX, 1990

Honda built the first Japanese plant in the US and took a stake in Rover for the production of badge-engineered cars in the UK. Nissan opened the doors to its factory in Tennessee in 1983. Toyota followed in 1984 with NUMMI, a joint venture with General Motors in Freemont, California. Together with their production facilities, the Japanese also exported their design offices—again a world-first move. In 1990, MIT researchers published the very influential book *The Machine that Changed the World*. Less then 30 years after the Japanese had entered the business, the automotive universe was given a choice: either to copy them or die. With Japan pioneering first the soft and later on the carved shape, both of which looked strikingly new to 1990s eyes, this became true even for design.

Designed and made in the United States, the Toyota Camry and Honda Accord alternated as best selling car in the US from 1997 onwards.

With a hybrid shape of iconic appeal—technologically dictated by the Californian Zero Emission Vehicle Act—the second generation Prius of 2003 was universally acclaimed as the green car of the future, its design univocally considered advanced. But in the new millennium, the Japanese mainframe was also confronted with an emerging new Asia. First South Korea, then China entered the competition. In doing so, they chose different business strategies—export and domestic-oriented respectively—but adopting the Japanese approach to car design. With Japan having turned car design into a global issue over the last twenty years of the modern century, a geographically united East Asia had become the epicenter of the car design world by the dawn of the global millennium.

NUMMI, 1989

Lexus ES 300, 1991

Acura Integra, 1986

Toyota Camry, 1986

Honda Accord 24S, 2002

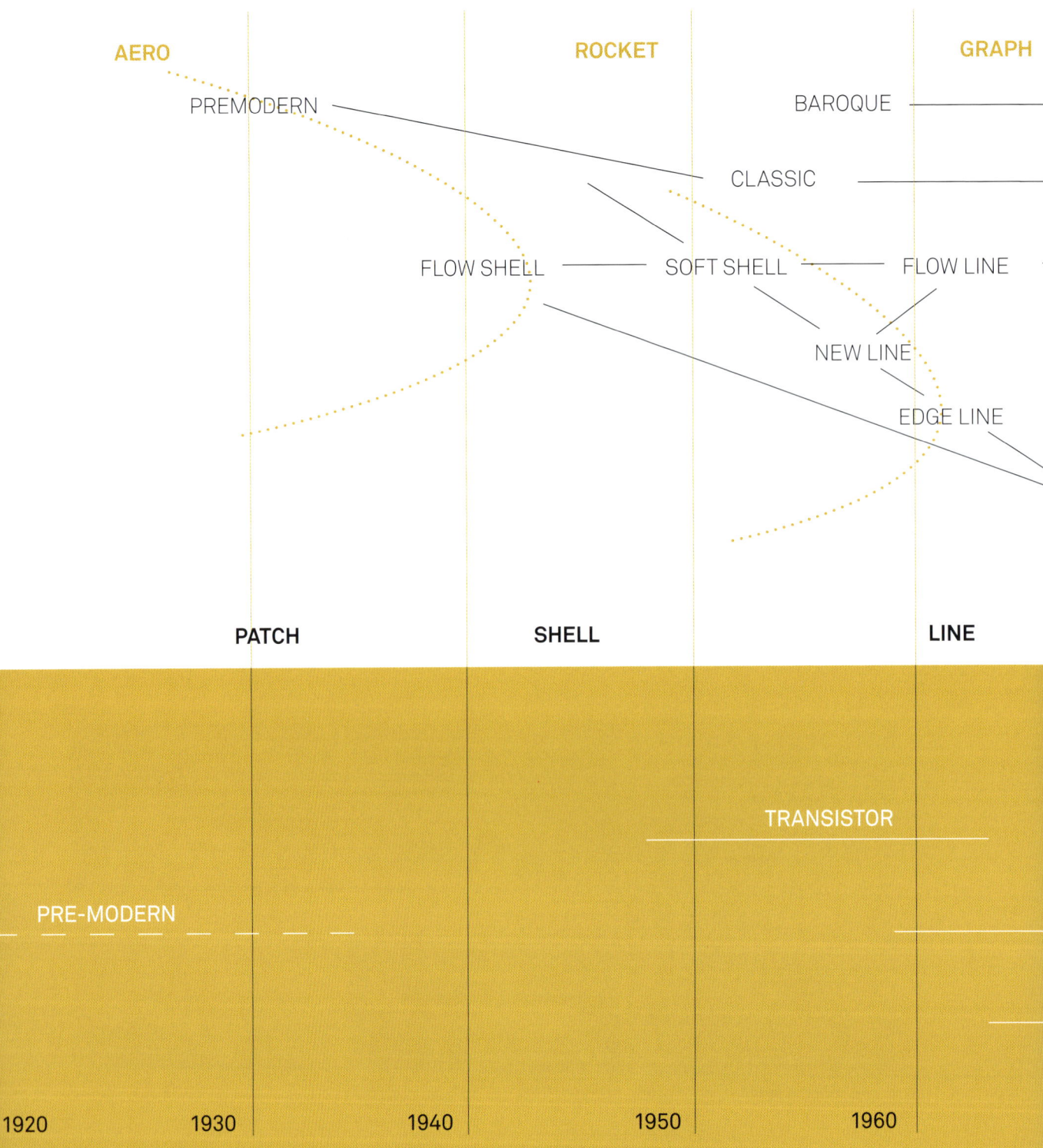
Paolo Tumminelli, Car Design: forms and themes 1920–2014

TRANSISTOR

On September 2, 1945 a state delegation, led by Minister of Foreign Affairs, Mamoru Shigemitsu, boarded the USS Missouri to sign the surrender agreement on behalf of Japan. The official ceremony appears to have been designed for the media. It is therefore not surprising that the Japanese showed up wearing the most formal of all Western attire, with their tall top hats posing as an obvious contradiction to the desolate state of both their country and soul. The effect was well planned: in comparison, uniformed General, Richard K. Sutherland, looked like a freshman in his fluffy pajamas. Incidentally, the ceremony was disturbed by a formal mistake: Canadian Colonel, Moore Cosgrave, signed the papers on the wrong line. The Japanese lamented this imperfection and accepted the document only after the Americans had repaired it—a small detail that ensured that the humiliation was now, at least in some way, reciprocal.

Once it had come to accept modernity, Japan chose to follow the Western example. After the West had thus physically penetrated Japan, it began dictating new rules of conduct, like an attempt at abolishing the *zaibatsu*, the original system upon which Japanese industry was based. Under these conditions, the Japanese tried hard to devise a unique car design language during the early 1950s. But not only was this a discipline that did not belong to their cultural capacities: competing with the styling masters was, quite plainly, as out of the question for the Japanese as it had been for a great many Western manufacturers. Back then, lesser brands simply followed fashion. For family cars that meant the pontoon line of Studebaker, for sports cars the Berlinetta line, as seen on the Cisitalia—both of 1947 vintage. While America provided the lifestyle to dream of, Italy was the place to go to for vanguard styling. Car design really worked like the fashion business of a Christian Dior: one went to the most fashionable of the automobile salons—Geneva, Paris, or Turin—to catch a glimpse of new, exciting lines. Those with high ambitions, enough money, and a minimum of manners then straightaway went ahead and hired the services of the great names

Toyopet Corona, 1957

from Turin and Milan. All others simply copied them. If this was the way to go in Europe, Japan could hardly ignore it.

ZEROCOPY

When production was resumed at the end of the 1940s, MITI, the mighty Ministry for International Trade and Industry, introduced strong but simple rules, aimed at regulating the automobile market in Japan. In the 1951 Road Vehicle Act, three groups of cars were identified. The *kei* car, with a cubic capacity of up to 0.36 liters, a maximum length of 3 and a width of 1.3 meters—later increased to 0.66 liters and 3.4 x 1.48 meters—enjoyed tax advantages and ownership privileges. Then, the Small Car segment, including all designs—even roadsters and vans—with a capacity of up to 2 liters or up to 4.7 meters in length. Finally, the Normal Car, which, in fact, would remain quite the exception until 1985, whose maximum size limits—below 5 meters—or power output—below 280 hp—varied over the years. Partnerships with Western manufacturers were enforced, leading to foreign models being imported as knock-down sets, to be assembled in Japan. The price the West had to pay to access this otherwise protected market was to enable a transfer of design know-how. Thus, Isuzu chose the Hillman Minx, Hino the Renault 4CV and Nissan the Austin A40 Somerset as their first all-new post-war cars. The implementation of unitary body construction then became the Japanese manufacturers' major struggle. Before the tie-ups, most bodies for Toyota, Datsun, and Isuzu had been made by Mitsubishi. At the beginning of the '50s, the design department at Nissan comprised just 15 people, with engineer, Teiichi Hara, alone in charge of body design—not to forget styling, of course. This shows in the modest simplicity of

USS Missouri, 1945

Toyopet SA, 1947

Datsun 1000, 1958

the Austin-based 1955 Datsun PL110, a design of Issigonian straightforwardness: just compare the exposed door hinges and the no-frills treatment of the front with the later Mini. Yet despite immediately winning the Mainichi Design Prize, it was called "the ugliest thing ever seen" when it approached the US in 1958 in the guise of the slightly modified Datsun 1000. As if to confirm a rather edgy attitude, Yutaka Katayama, at the time Nissan's man in the US, is on the record declaring: "The car itself is not a kind of porcelain... we are not selling the body. We are selling the efficiency of the car." Only Toyota seemingly bypassed the invitation to team up and chose the 'learning by doing' approach instead—which obviously included a careful analysis of what the West was doing. The result was the 1955 Toyopet Crown—the nickname given to the SA model had become Toyota's official brand in 1949. Not only was this car a modern pontoon design with unitary body construction, it also obviously followed the European recipe for the family sedan with its downsized American style.

The new Toyopet's in-house styling was charming, its detailing generous, and the front grille treatment—some kind of chrome ribbon—unique enough to lend the car some identity. The crimson Crown badge on the front clearly indicated the ambitions of the company, if not of the country itself. Accompanied by an equally charming Miss Japan, the new car was sent to the US in 1957, where it was acclaimed as a "baby Cadillac." However, this initial enthusiasm was soon to evaporate. After road tests in Los Angeles had proven to be a disaster, the Crown simply would not sell. When Toyota Motor Inc. finally asked a Ford executive for help, he called the thing "underpowered and overpriced" and complained about the brand name: "Toy sounds like a toy, and toys break... pet sounds like your dog."

Datsun Fairlady, 1959

Toyopet Crown, 1957

Toyopet Crown, 1957

BONSAI

The export ambitions of both the Datsun and the Crown reveal the weakness of the Japanese market. Except for taxi companies and a few officials, the public could hardly afford a car. In 1955, production was still very low at 20,268 vehicles—two thirds of which were accounted for by Toyota and Nissan— prompting the MITI to arrange a competition for the project of a Japanese "National Car." However, its brief was more challenging than convincing: engine size between 0.35 and half a liter, room for two to four people and a load of 100 kg, top speed above 100 kph, and consumption as low as 3.33 liters, at an average of 60 kph—and all this for the ridiculous price of 250,000 yen. But while this project was unsurprisingly never realized, it actually boosted the design departments of all manufacturers, which were soon developing new models, specifically conceived for the Japanese market. And what a wonderfully creative phase this turned out to be! Rather than following a standard, each brand opted for an altogether different design strategy. The minimal 1957 Suzulight was clearly inspired by the German Lloyd, but added—in the commercial version—a very practical tailgate. Fuji Heavy Industries launched the Subaru 360 in 1958, whose rounded, flowing lines were a very personal interpretation of the small car theme established by the Fiat 500. Along the way, the 360 also set the standard for the *kei* car, the most exquisitely Japanese of all car design concepts.

Frighteningly small, these little cars competed—albeit not in terms of plain performance—for superiority in lightweight construction, engine technology and style. Although initially a surrogate for the not yet affordable "small car," this typology rapidly developed into a very intelligent form of individual micromobility. With design

Subaru 360, 1958

Suzuki Suzulight SS, 1955

Suzuki Fronte 360, 1967

Mitsubishi 500, 1959

Suzuki Carry Van, 1967

variations ranging from sedan to minivan, from coupé to roadster, spotting a farm with several *kei* cars parked in front of it—one for each family member—became an everyday sight. Their popularity rapidly increased through 1970, when more than 750,000 units were produced. Yet, in spite of the attempt to boost sales with a new engine displacement of 0.55 liters, the reduction of usage benefits caused a reverse trend from 1975 onwards and all the way through the bubbling eighties. But due to the recession of the 1990s, and thanks to a new displacement limit of 0.66 liters—with the power output limit raised to a stratospheric 64 hp—these bonsai style, often supercharged exotics became the largest market segment from 1999 onwards, with new registrations remaining stable in the region of 1.5 million. Almost as if they wanted to keep the best for themselves, the Japanese never seriously attempted to sell the *kei* cars in overcrowded Europe, thereby turning the most charming of them—the Honda Z or the Suzuki Cappuccino—into a sort of exclusive classics.

MANGA

In 1960 the Toyo Kogyo Company—today's Mazda—entered the lightweight car market with its first four-wheeler, the R360 Coupé, whose cheerful elegance vaguely reminds of the Cinquecento's sister, the Autobianchi Bianchina. What are most eye-catching about Mazda's *kei* car are its fancy eyes—whose generous chrome rims of asymmetrical shape emphasize the little car's glance, lending it a human-like character. It is hard not to spot the reference to the first manga, Osamu Tezuka's *Tetsuwan Atom*—known all over the globe as Astro Boy. The little robot with iron arms and those trademark big eyes (originally inspired by Betty Boop) was launched in 1952, instigating the global appeal of later anime

Astro Boy, 1950s

Mazda P360 Carol, 1962

characters. Similar manga eyelashes enhanced not only the otherwise inconspicuous design of the Mitsubishi 500 of 1959, but have since established themselves as one of the major design features of Japanese cars.

Compared with these smart mini vehicles, Toyota's national car for 1960, purposely named Publica, was comparatively upscale, despite having much less of an impact in terms of style. While its overall design themes recall the *trapèze* line of European fashion, its detailing is very *wabi*—reassuringly humble in its diminutive application of chrome. In choosing the name Contessa—Italian for countess—Hino demonstrated even clearer upscale ambitions for its family car. Despite its technology being based on the rear-engined Renault, its design, officially of Japanese origin, is reminiscent of a Triumph Herald, a BMW 700, or the obvious Renault Floride. The difficulty of appreciating Japanese cars of the early 1960s is what appears to be a certain acerbity about their design: be it the squeezed proportions or the rough modeling or the fancy details—the composition certainly struggled to reach the levels of maturity of its Western counterparts, which in those days were considered exemplary. Moving further upscale, a new Toyopet Corona was brought along in 1960, with a semblance of a cleaned-up, smoothed down Opel Rekord of Euro-American fashion, as well as a new Nissan Cedric, remotely reminiscent of an Austin Westminster. To call them copies would be unjust though: the Toyopet introduced the peculiarly dynamic, slanting doors cut, which was to become a trademark of later Coronas; the Nissan features a full width front grille with enclosed twin headlamps, which was innovative even by European standards.

Nissan Cedric, 1960

Toyopet Coronaline Van, 1960

Hino Contessa 900, 1961

TOKYORINO

The design relationship between Japan and Italy really is a kind of love story. Coming to Italy for the 1960 Olympics on a motorbike world tour, journalist, Hideyuki Miyakawa, fell in love with beautiful Marisa, married her, and decided to stay. Having recognized the creative potential of the three big *carrozzieri*—Bertone, Ghia, and Pininfarina—he established himself as a kind of secret agent of design. His first assignment was the design of a new sedan for Toyo Kogyo, the 1965 Luce 1500, which was to be executed by Bertone. There, young Miyakawa got to know young Giugiaro, with whom he would later collaborate on behalf of Isuzu, Toyota, Nissan, Suzuki, and Hyundai. In the wake of this Italian wave, Pininfarina was hired by Nissan for the 1965 Cedric, Vignale worked for Daihatsu on the Compagno line, and Giovanni Michelotti on assignments for Prince and Hino. Despite their classic *Torinese* heritage, these Italo-Japanese designs really betray an in-between style of their own, for which there may have been several reasons. Firstly, due to being an emerging industry, the Japanese body building skills were not comparable with those of the Europeans. Secondly, the Japanese market of the 1960s was still quite conservative, accounting for rather unexceptional lines. Thirdly, the squeezed body proportions obviously resulted in a different stance. Fourthly and lastly: the cultural gap influencing as delicate and complex a process as car design—for the Italians, perfectly attuned to their very own design slang and Piedmontese dialect, communicating with the Japanese must have been a nightmare. While this design connection has always remained active, the Japanese were actually most eager to benefit from shared knowledge and learn, rather than simply import a style.

Daihatsu Compagno, 1963

Daihatsu Compagno Station Wagon, 1963   Prince Skyline Sport coupé, 1962

Toyota Publica, 1961

Transistor 28

Prince Skyline 1500, 1957

Prince Skyline 1500 Deluxe, 1966

PRINCE

It comes as little surprise that Prince, having emerged from the Tachikawa Aircraft Company and being run by aircraft engineers, built among the finest cars of its time. The Skyline and Gloria sedans are not just well-designed and prestigious, but also incorporated quite a few innovations that are not found on other Japanese cars of the 1950s and '60s, such as six cylinder engines and de Dion rear suspension. Thanks to its quality and prestige, the Prince marque is not just associated with the Japanese Imperial Court in name only—in 1967, it actually builds a limousine for the Royal Household. This air of excellence seems to be at odds with Japan's culture, which poses a challenge for this rather small purveyor of fine, if not subversively elitist automobiles. Unlike the West, where Mercedes-Benz, Cadillac, or Jaguar are revered, Japan cultivated a schizophrenic attitude towards prestige. So after Nissan took over in 1968, the proud Prince was sentenced to disappear, while his heirs, the Skyline and Gloria badges, were kept alive.

Prince Skyline 2000 GT, 1965

Prince Gloria, 1962
Prince 1900 Sprint, 1963

Hino Contessa 900 Sprint, 1962

Hino Contessa 900, 1961

HINO

A model range bearing the fancy name of Contessa—Italian for Countess—is all that remains of the short-lived adventure of Hino Motors as a producer of passenger cars. It all started in 1953, when Hino joined forces with Renault, in order to assemble the popular 4CV. Renault's rear engine configuration gave the 1961 Contessa, a small sedan of European appeal, a unique identity within the Japanese panorama. Out of its sturdy body, Giovanni Michelotti conjured a 'dashing spectacle' in the shape of the 900 Sprint version—"Japan's Grand Design" remaining reserved to the Japanese market. Last and least of all came two larger, more fashionable Contessa 1300 models, a sedan and a coupé by Michelotti, which must be regarded as the Japanese Corvair: equally unfortunate and exotic. Following the MITI's call for strategic alliances among manufacturers, Hino reinvented itself in 1966 as the truck and bus specialist within the Toyota group.

Hino Contessa 1300, 1964

Nissan Cedric Special, 1964

Nissan Cedric Custom Six, 1963

Mazda Familia, 1964

Mazda Familia Van, 1963

Subaru 1000, 1965

Isuzu Florian 1600 Deluxe, 1967

Mitsubishi Minica, 1962

KEI CAR

The *kei jidōsha* creation was one of the more blatant cases of Japanese politics exerting influence over the automotive sector. The agenda was twofold: to stimulate domestic car development, production and sales, as well as to establish means of private transport the country's crowded metropolises could cope with. Fiscal incentives for buyers convinced the manufacturers to come up with a wide range of lightweight cars, which combined the crude with the intricate. The early generation may have been a variation on the global post-war bubble car theme, but by the late 1960s, the second generation, spearheaded by the Honda N360 and Mitsubishi Minica, established the blueprint of what constituted the all-Japanese *kei* car: tiny size, peppy look, sporty drive, low cost. As if to prove that Japan actually is a different world, the *kei* car declares that even in cars, when it comes to style, size really does not matter.

Subaru 360 Young SS, 1968

Mazda R360, 1960

Suzuki Fronte, 1973

Suzuki Fronte, 1969

Honda NIII 360 Touring Deluxe, 1970

Mitsubishi Minica Deluxe, 1970

Mazda Luce 1500, 1965

HIDEYUKI MIYAKAWA

Coming to Rome for the Summer Olympics in 1960, motorcycle globetrotter Hideyuki Miyakawa fell in love not just with the country, but with one of its most charming citizens: Marisa, a Japan and car enthusiast, who also counted Italian arts among her interests. The couple first met at the Automobile Show in Turin, where the young gentleman finally saw the light. Employing a canny approach, he convinced Toyo Kogyo to have Bertone design their new small car, called Luce, Italian for light. Miyakawa soon realized that not Nuccio Bertone, but his employee Giorgetto Giugiaro was the go-to designer. The two young men and Marisa then travelled across Japan together, giving birth to both the known design work for Isuzu—including the dream car come true Piazza—Mazda, Nissan, Subaru, Suzuki and Toyota, as well as several other love children. Later, the trio repeated the trick in South Korea with Hyundai. A one-of-a-kind secret agent of design, Miyakawa has been the catalyst of a global design culture. One where East meets West, with mutual enjoyment and respect.

Mitsubishi Colt 1100, 1966

Mitsubishi New Colt Custom 1200, 1968

Mitsubishi Colt 1000 Van, 1963
Mitsubishi New Colt 1500 Wagon Deluxe, 1968

Mazda Familia 1200 Coupé, 1968

Mazda Familia 1000 Deluxe, 1967

Isuzu Bellett, 1973

Isuzu Bellett, 1963

Toyota Publica, 1969

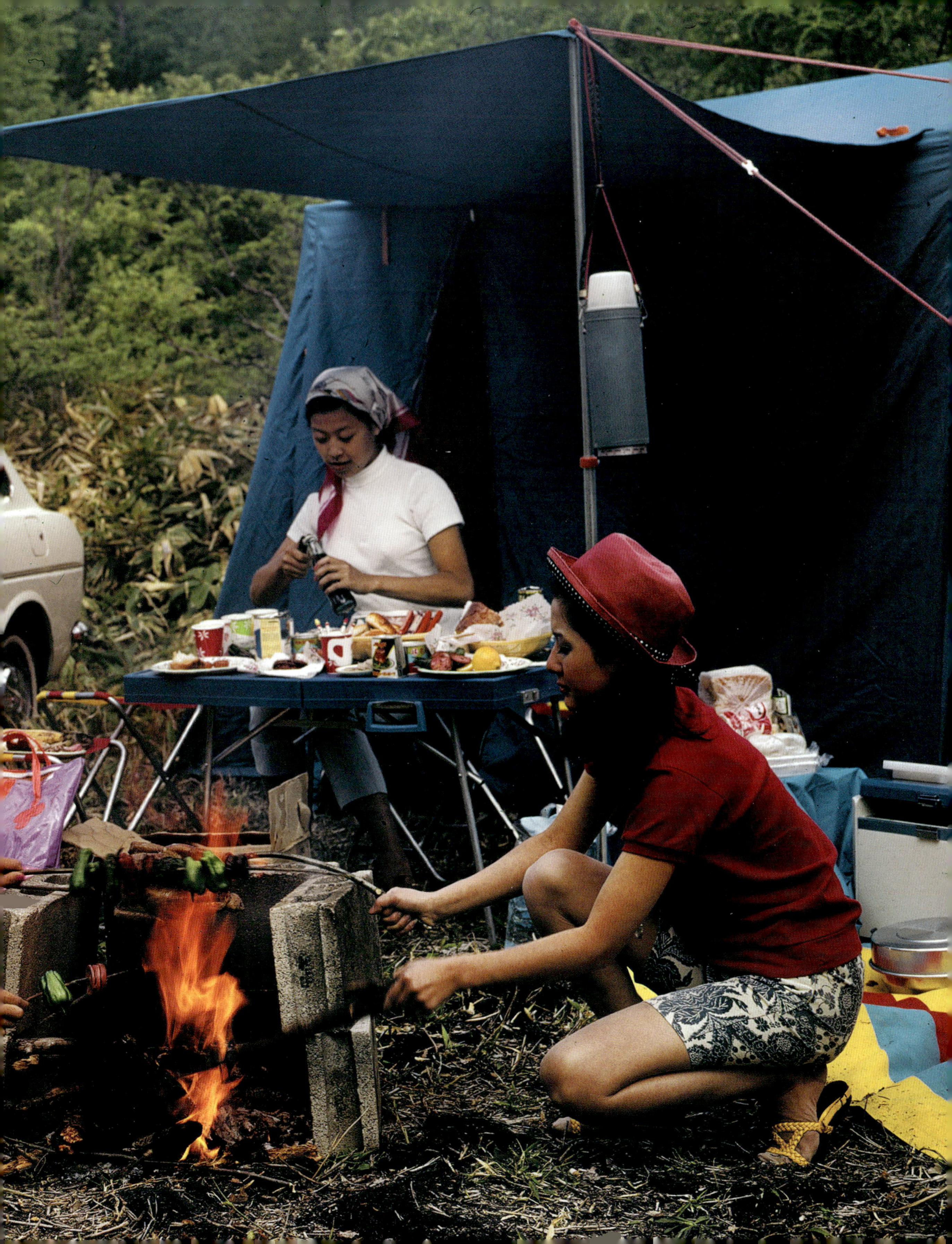

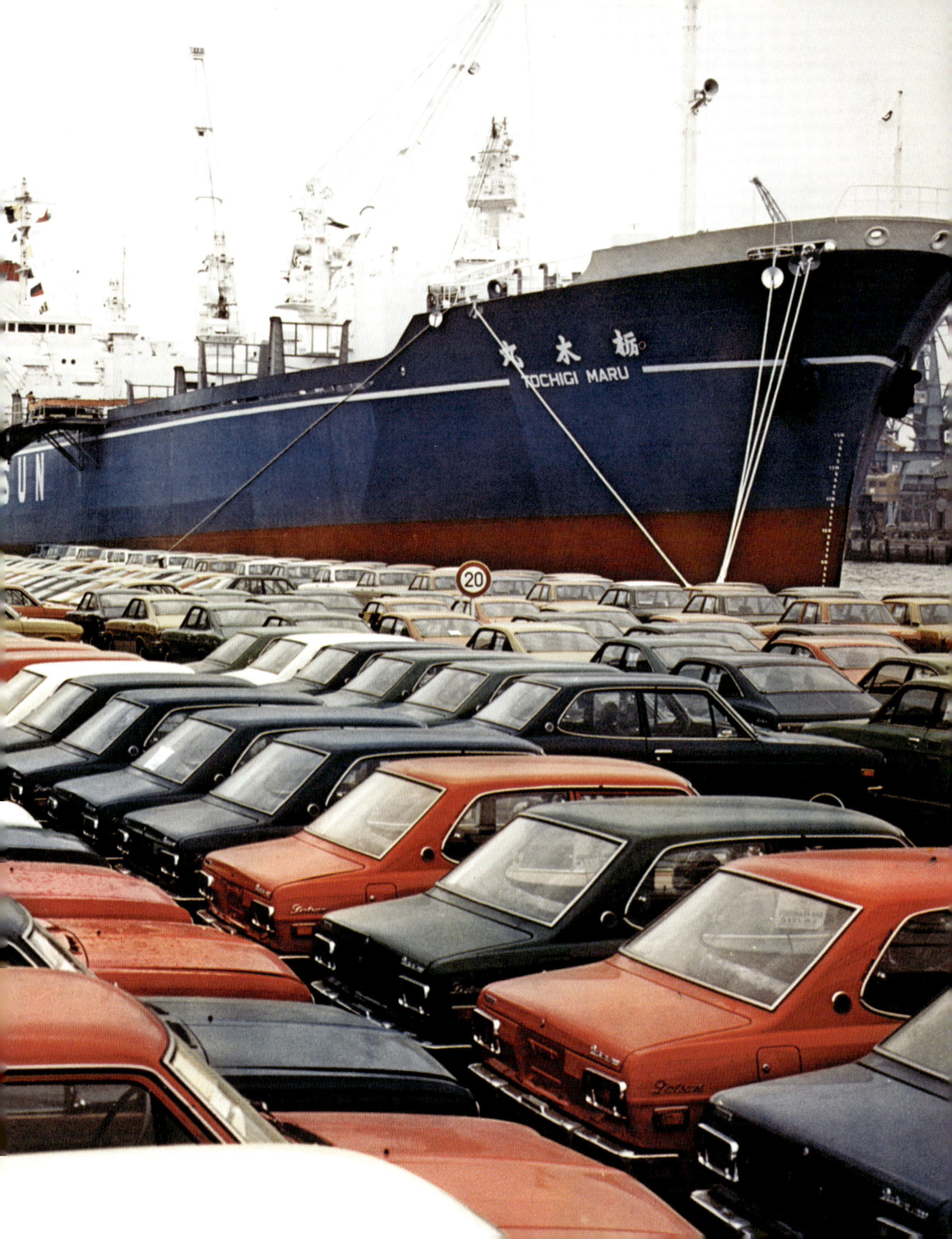
栃木丸
TOCHIGI MARU
20

JAP AM

Soon after having opened up to the West, Japan substituted the kimono for Savile Row. The traditional Japanese dress code would have hardly been understood in a Western business environment anyway. Donald Richie explains that, traditionally, the kimono only comes in two sizes, male and female. It is barely designed to fit the wearer, the wearer being designed to fit it instead. Richie mentions "individual conformity": "Each city, each house and each person is different from all the others, yet essentially the same." The kimono means harmony through uniformity, making all individuals feel part of one group. Even behavior and movements are designed—or better: directed—by the layers of cloth, carefully folded to build up into one protective shell. The inner core is never visible, nor does the kimono enhance the typical spotlights of western fashion: the breasts, the hips, the *derrière*. It is the torso that pops out, that most solid aspect of the human body. And even though the rigidity of the kimono is reflected in the strength of the formal Western suit, its looks are not. So when the dark grey suit became their new uniform, the Japanese *sararīmen*, white-collar managers of Western ambitions, needed an outer shell—the automobile—designed with the same degree of harmonious uniformity. As Richie says about urbanity in Japan: "In Europe, one is part of the display—to see and to be seen, to look and to be looked at. The street is a stage. How different Japan." Here, the walker is not an actor, rather he is an active spectator: "The street is the show, the display. The Japanese street is very public, conversely, the Japanese home is very private." On Sunday afternoons, the busiest streets at the focal points of the capital used to be closed to motor traffic, for the people to invade the road like they used to do, back in the old days. The corso of American Graffiti, the car demonstratively parked on suburbia's driveways, the showing off in front of the cafés on French and Italian piazzas—in Japan, there was simply no room for any of this. The automobile would not change that. In a way, the Japanese "small car"—as MITI used to brand the family sedan—was analogous to its Western counterparts, and yet

Datsun's Tochigi Maru, 1971

utterly different. The first misunderstanding stems from the style *vis à vis* size relationship. In terms of dimensions, the Japanese had no better option than to choose the European style packaging. But from a design and marketing standpoint, they firmly had the United States in mind—their very first and most important export market. Thus inspired by American fashion, but European in spirit, the Japanese car of the sixties is a unique blend of European mainstream and American kitsch. But this in itself is nothing new really, as the same design strategy was also being pursued by many contemporary European models, especially those made by Ford and General Motors in England and Germany.

But while America and Europe had a similar stylistic cultural background, Japan and the West were simply incompatible. Japan's nature-related sensibility actually prohibits geometrical symmetry and refuses the romance of *façades*. It accepts kitsch without having a word for it, while at the same time venerating all things modular—think tatami. In fact, within this sense of harmony, a fundamental contradiction can be observed. For not even the Japanese writing system is univocal, but based on three coexisting scripts: *kanji* is derived from Chinese logograms and used for the basics, *hiragana* is used for verbs, adjectives and grammatical particles, and *katakana* employed for, among others, foreign names. Although thoroughly permeated by a Shintoistic naturalism, by that sense of "transience and impermanence" observed by Richie, the "Japanese have been modern for the last ten centuries," as French poet, Henri Michaux, put it in 1932, while appreciating the structural functionalism of the traditional Japanese home. But then the misunderstandings begin, with the incompatibility of the aesthetic vocabulary. Japan actually has no word for aesthetics—so *bigaku* was invented as late as 1883, in

Miss Fairlady, Ginza 1964

Nissan's Summer Olympic showroom at Ginza, 1964

order to translate the German theories of *Ästhetik*. Even the basic tastes are not comparable: the West knew four (sweet, sour, salty, and bitter), but Japan added at least four: delicacy, deliciousness, astringency, and acridity. With all this in mind, transforming Japanese thoughts into Western words—and the other way around—never quite seemed to work without getting somewhat lost in translation.

In 1961, MITI revealed plans to reorganize the manufacturers, in order to achieve even greater competitiveness. The result was a new structure: Toyota, taking Hino and Daihatsu into its group, and Nissan, absorbing Prince and tied up with Fuji Heavy Industries, qualified as the only mass producers with a full vehicle range. Another group consisted of smaller companies related to US manufacturers: Mitsubishi & Chrysler, Isuzu & General Motors, Toyo Kogyo & Ford. To this last group belonged two independent companies, both originating from the two-wheeler sector: Honda and Suzuki.

During this process, Nissan and Toyota expanded their lineup for the purpose of venturing into the domestic and export markets. Both brands developed a unique personality along the way. Nissan obtained technological leadership and international flair, while Toyota stood for uncompromising quality and Japanese values. Their respective naming policies clearly underline these differing approaches. As Nissan's eternal president, Katsuji Kawamata, was in love with America, the cars were given names such as Datsun Bluebird (as sung in *Over the Rainbow*) and Fairlady (from the musical *My Fair Lady*) or Nissan Cedric (citing the hero of *Little Lord Fauntleroy*). Similarly, Toyota just could not get rid of its association with the most royal accessory after the Crown sedan, named in Crown Prince Akihito's honor. A Tiara (the Pope's crown), a Corona (Italian for crown)

Ginza, 1970

and a Corolla (the petal crown of a flower) consequently followed, leading up to the 1980s, when the Camry—standing for *kanmuri*, Japanese for crown—arrived. Slowly but surely, competition between the Big Two escalated into an all-out marketing battle: the long-lasting BC war between Bluebird and Corona for the crown of best-selling passenger car in Japan, a heritage still felt today. With the new model years of their small cars, 1963 and 1964 respectively, the Japanese finally entered the global competition. The Bluebird S310 sported a neat design by Pininfarina, which would have had her compete head-to-head with the handsome Lancia Fulvia. To suit the smart dress image as well as Nissan's sports ambitions, SS and SSS versions with up to 90 hp were soon made available. As if to underline its more sedate, almost austere design, Toyota's Corona was test driven over 100,000 kilometers on the Mieshin Expressway, Japan's first motorway, inaugurated in 1963. The Corona was utterly modern, anticipating the sleek international style of the Fiat 124. Compared to the European world car, the Japanese had much finer surface modeling and more sophisticated trim details, including a full-width front grille with generous twin headlamps. The next generation Bluebird for 1967, having grown out of Pininfarina's design, was even more up to date by any standards and turned into the first Japanese global hit.

These finally were cars the Americans were happy to buy! Between 1960 and 1965, exports consequently skyrocketed: Nissan's from 4,500 to almost 40,000, Toyota's from 1,800 to just above 33,000. And if those numbers do not impress enough, the export figures for 1970, which, supported by the new Corolla and Sunny of 1966, were multiplied again by factor seven for Nissan and by factor ten for Toyota, should do the trick.

Fiat 124, 1966

Toyota Corona, 1964

Datsun Sunny, 1966

Datsun Bluebird, 1963

Datsun Bluebird, 1967

Toyota Corolla, 1966

AMERICANHIT

With their unique two-door notchback body, the Corolla and Sunny were just as similar in concept as they were different in style. The Datsun's was more of a crisp, European fit, and would have stood up well alongside an Opel Kadett or Fiat 128—as well as a Chevrolet Nova or a Dodge Dart. The Toyota—for which, finally, the Toyopet name had been abandoned—featured a more individual design, characterized by flowing lines and a carefully modeled front end with sophisticated chrome work and a hint of manga eyes. At the other end of the spectrum, with 6 and 8 cylinder engines and at a length of 4.7 meters, the Toyota Crown and Crown Eight had almost grown up into American full-size sedans: lots of chrome, a hint of fins and heavy side panel modeling being obvious clues. Their counterparts were the equally upmarket Prince Gloria and Grand Gloria. When seen in a side mirror, both models could have easily been mistaken for a contemporary Buick. That being said, one should not be so foolish and expect any less of an American look from Mitsubishi's top-of-the-line marque, the dignified Debonair.

The Japanese lineup had not yet reached its completion: 1965 saw the arrival of Nissan's flagship limousine, for whose name Kawamata's immediate choice once again turned out to be a very American one: President. Toyota's reaction arrived in 1967 and going by the similarly predictable name of Century—commemorating the Meiji Era's centennial. With confidence growing, not just the number of models increased, but their designs swelled too, becoming as American as can be in the process: featuring orgiastic chrome grilles, the inevitable hard tops, fancy opera windows, coke bottle or equally imaginative sidelines. This may have had beneficial effects on business,

Toyopet Crown, 1962

Prince Gloria, 1962

Toyopet Crown Wagon, 1962

as the US market seemed to appreciate a more economical car only if it offered no less glam than the domestic choice. There is obviously no denying the logic of this tactic, as it saw more than a twentyfold increase in production, from 165,000 units in 1960 to almost 4.5 million in 1975.

Rushing through the 1970s and towards the 1980s and global leadership, the standard style of the Japanese lost all traces of European taste. Aesthetically hyperventilating, overloaded with chrome, rich in creative paraphernalia—yet still one size too small for a gold medal—it was heading for the direction of the new baroque—or the simply odd—of American fashion instead. Japanese design was most certainly targeting right at the core of the US market. The myth of the *kenmeri* Skyline was built around TV spots featuring a mellow teen model couple, Ken and Mary—a nice girl of Caucasian-Californian descent and an exotic, half-Russian, half-Japanese boy. Of the first Skyline, with its iconic four round tail lamps, more than 600,000 were built over the course of four years, or twice as many as of the legendary previous model. It also happened to be by far outselling the Fiat 131 Mirafiori, the best-selling midsize sedan, built by Europe's largest manufacturer. It was not without a reason that American critic, Brock Yates, called the 1972 Honda Civic "the most brilliant small car in automotive history." Its subcompact size and cutting edge emission control CVCC technology in fact made it the first successful Honda in the US, with one million sold over the first four years. Yet judging its design through European eyes, this actually appeared to be a rather old-fashioned piece of metalwork, compared with the contemporary Volkswagen. But that does not distract from the rationality behind this following of American trends, considering Japanese car production output was shared by almost 50–50 between domestic and

Nissan Laurel, 1977

Toyota Crown Royal Saloon, 1979

Nissan Skyline hardtop coupé *kenmeri*, 1972

export sales, which might explain why the radically innovative wedge line, which hit Turin in 1968 and quickly spread across Europe through to 1978, received almost no appreciation among the Japanese, who remained tied to the conservative American styling for a prolonged period.

CRUISE CONTROL

Where the Japanese accepted no compromise was in Total Quality Control. This included such efforts as supporting the establishment of the J.D. Power Customer Satisfaction Index, which would become one of the major driving forces in terms of consumer orientation. Obedient as they were, the Japanese also followed the 1966 National Traffic and Motor Vehicle Safety Act to the letter, implementing a very strict recall system, thus expressing that they really did care for their customers. As Koichi Shimokawa points out, the shy Japanese had gradually evolved into an industry "characterized by a multiple product-focus production philosophy, (…) based on low volumes, tightly linked to changes in market structure." Frequent design changes were thus possible, just like the very flexible production of many design variations of similar models for different markets. Reviewing today the most exemplary designs of 1965–75, one cannot help but smile at the vivid imagination and the astonishing strangeness of many design solutions. The Japanese car may have set the new standard for the global mass market car, and in doing so, it also grew to be as kitschy as a car could possibly get. But then again, is that not what meeting global taste is all about? The Japanese cars may not have been the world's fastest, but, at this point, their design already was.

Honda Civic, 1972

Nissan Cherry F-II estate, 1974

Datsun Bluebird SSS hardtop coupé, 1976

Mitsubishi Debonair Executive, 1970

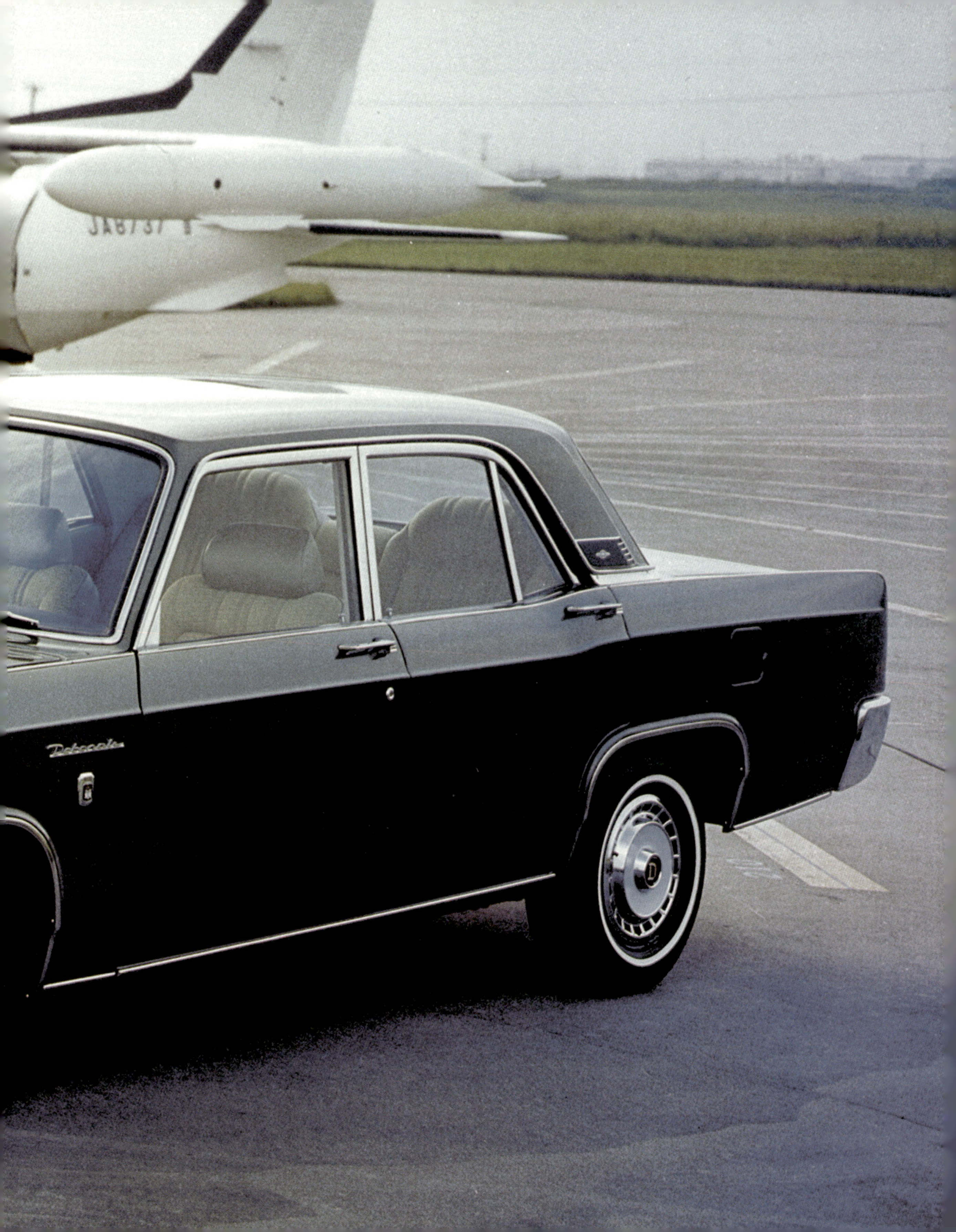

Datsun Bluebird 1300, 1963

DATSUN

Entering the US passenger car market in 1958, Nissan's name carried some undesirable connotations, such as having been associated with the armaments industry during the Second World War. Datsun—originally for the "son" of car maker Dat—on the other hand, was unburdened and soon made a name for itself in the US as a maker of sturdy small cars. In 1968, not just customers, but also the competition took note of the 510 Series Datsun Bluebird. This was as thoroughly modern a compact sedan as one would have expected from a European manufacturer—think BMW's *Neue Klasse*. In fact, Datsun had cultivated an international approach towards product development long before it became common sense among the entire industry. Catering to a foreign market by offering tailor-made products, rather than trying to sell an indigenous product to foreigners, lent Datsun an advantage in the crucial American market, where its seminal Fairlady Z sports coupé was in a class of its own. The mainstay Bluebird range of sedans, however, had to fight off a potent adversary in the shape of Toyota's Corona. This conflict—or, as some referred to it, war—between two sedans was about nothing less than supremacy among the Big Two Japanese car makers.

Datsun Bluebird 1600 SSS, 1968

Toyopet Corona, 1964

Toyota Corona Mark II, 1967

Toyota Crown Super Saloon *kujira*, 1971

Toyota Crown Super Deluxe Hardtop *kujira*, 1971

Toyota Corolla, 1966

TOYOTA

Toyota has long since transcended the status of a mere corporate giant. It is a method-turned-ideology—one could even say a mythology—of the modern industrial age: the Toyota Way, also known as the Japanese Way. Steeped in tradition, the family business conquered the world less through assimilation, then by adapting a mindset that is quintessentially Japanese. *Kaizen*, continuous improvement, and *jidoka*, enabling any worker to stop a production line in case a problem occurs, is the means through which Toyota has set the benchmark in build quality, *kanban* is the precursor of the ubiquitous just-in-time production strategy. Success through consistent pursuit of Japanese ideals also distinguishes Toyota's products, which can be characterized as traditional—if not merely decent—in more ways than one. Exceptions, whenever available—such as the 2000 GT—never were the rule. Toyota shares its appreciation of decency with the conservative middle classes. It is the ordinary people the Corollas and Crowns are designed for. While the Toyota logo on the trunk reassures them—and everybody else—a populuxe model badge on the front grille cheers the driver's ambitions on. Just like the two billion people who were said to watch William and Kate's wedding ceremony, the king of car manufacturers pays its respects to the higher power, the Emperor, ten million times a year.

EIJI TOYODA

There would be no Toyota Way without Eiji Toyoda. In fact, there would be no Toyota as we know it—the world's largest car brand—without Eiji Toyoda. For it was he who first travelled to the US to study production methods at Ford's factories, before establishing mass production at the company of his cousin, Kiichiro. However, just copying Ford's assembly lines was not good enough for Eiji Toyoda, who established the much-praised and later copied Japanese way of making cars. With such towering achievements as *kaizen* and *kanban* to his credit, it appears almost marginal that Eiji also pushed Toyota into the automotive premiere league and championed the development of hybrid propulsion.

Toyota Century, 1967

Eiji Toyoda & Toyopet Crown, 1957

Jap Am

Nissan President V8E, 1973

Nissan Skyline Van 1500 DX, 1969

Nissan Skyline 1500 Deluxe, 1968

Datsun Cherry GL, 1970

Datsun Bluebird U GL, 1971

Nissan Cedric 2800 Brougham, 1975
Nissan Cedric 2800 Brougham hardtop, 1975

Honda 1300 coupé GL, 1970

Datsun Violet hardtop coupé, 1973

Datsun Cherry estate, 1973

Nissan Cherry Coupé GL, 1971

Datsun Sunny 1400 Excellent GL S coupé, 1973

Datsun Sunny 1200 S, 1973

Datsun Violet 1600 SSS, 1973

Mazda Luce Rotary RE 12, 1973

Nissan Skyline 2000 GTX-E, 1972

Nissan Skyline 2000 GTX-E, 1972

Nissan Skyline 2000 GT-X hardtop coupé *kenmeri*, 1972

Nissan Skyline 2000 GT-X, 1972

Nissan Skyline Deluxe 1800 Van, 1972

Mitsubishi Lancer, 1973

Mitsubishi Lancer Wagon, 1973

Mitsubishi Galant GL 1850 Hardtop, 1973

Mitsubishi Galant GSII 2000, 1975

MITSUBISHI

The offspring of the giant Mitsubishi Heavy Industries, Mitsubishi Motors wrote history by introducing Japan's first series production automobile in 1917. Based on the Fiat Tipo 3, its provenance proved to be visionary, for it established a pattern Mitsubishi abided by for almost a century to come. Penned by a former GM designer, the 1964 Debonair—one of three Japanese luxury liners—set itself apart with its Lincoln Continental look, and remained in production, virtually unchanged, for 22 years. Seeking cooperation agreements with other automotive manufacturers remained the cornerstone of Mitsubishi's policy, particularly during its 22-year association with Chrysler, which began in 1971.

This willingness to cater to international lifestyles has been a defining trait of Mitsubishi's over the years—from the 1978 Colt, a compact car with European appeal, through the Pajero off-roader and the Space Wagon van, to the Lancer Evolution rally fighter series—whose later iterations were designed by Pininfarina. Pioneering foreign markets, Mitsubishi succeeded thanks to its ability to adapt, somewhat to the detriment of an identifiable engineering or styling ethos. This lack of stylistic distinction eventually became a logical consequence of the status of the "three diamonds" as the least Japanese—if not the most eminently global—of all Japanese brands.

Mitsubishi Delica Coach, 1974

Mitsubishi Celeste, 1975

Toyota Hi-Lux Half Ton, 1973

Datsun 620 Cab Truck, 1976

Toyota Celica GT, 1970

Toyota Celica ST Liftback, 1976

Toyota Chaser SGS, 1978

Toyota Celica XX, 1978

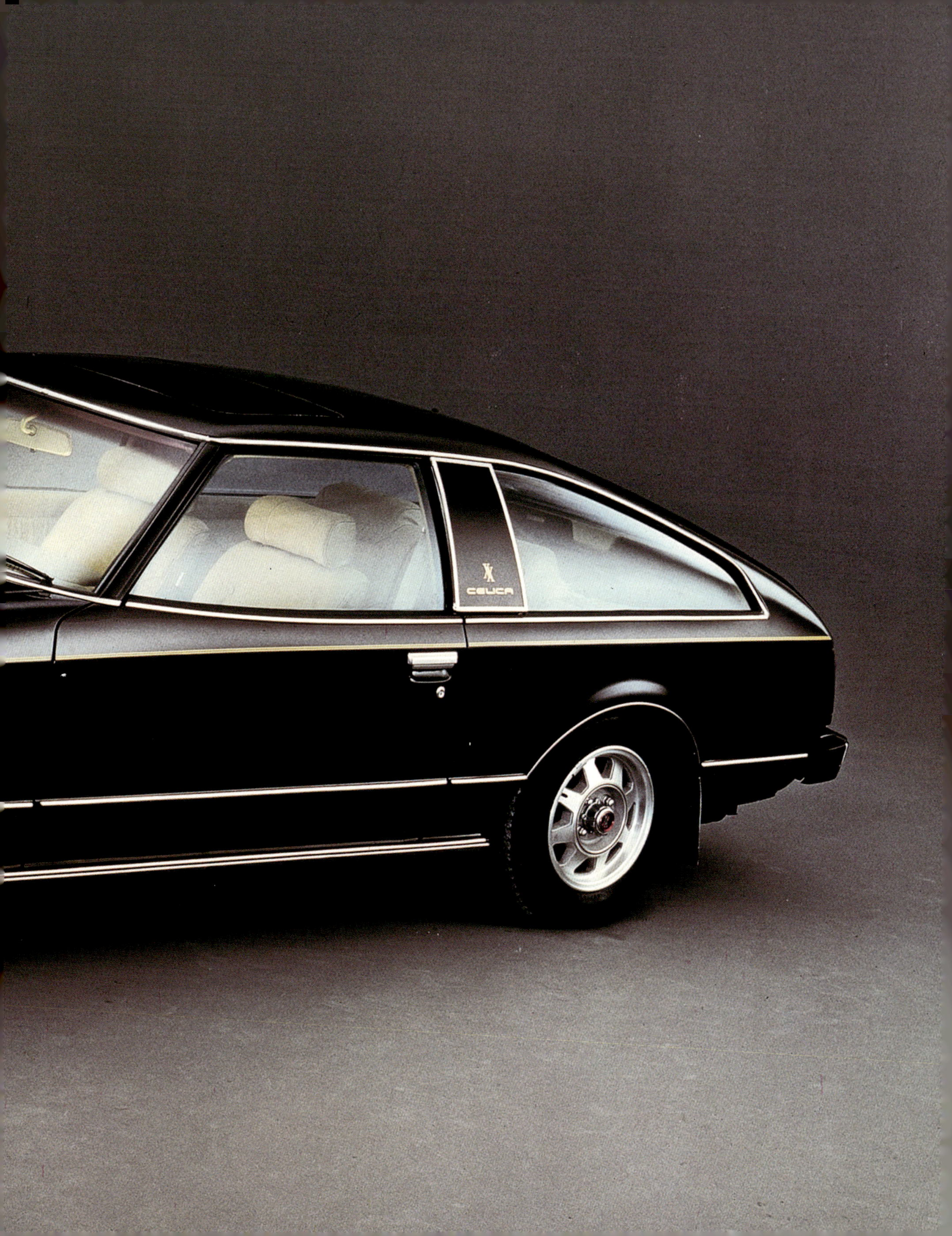
CELICA

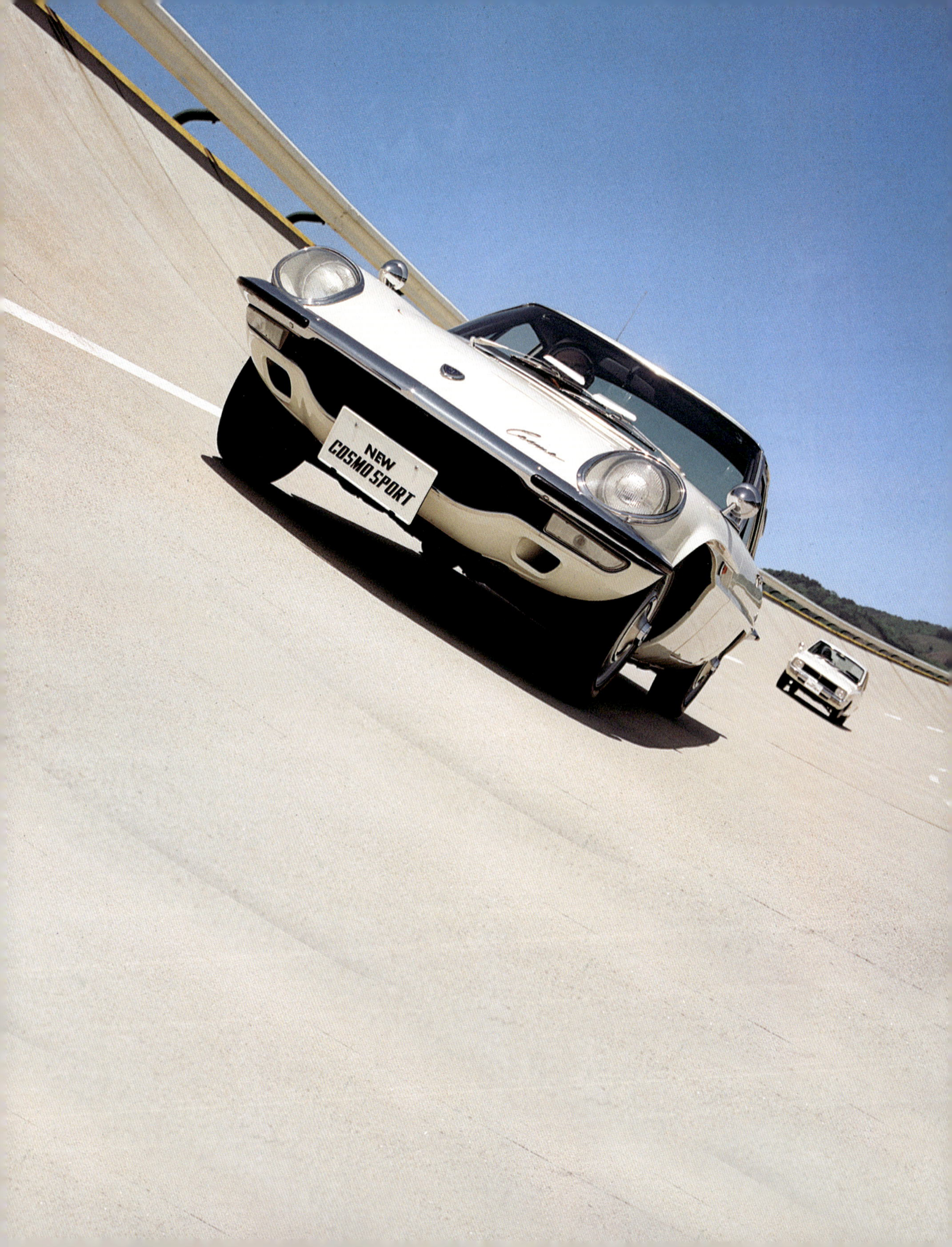
NEW
COSMO SPORT

IKONIK

Two decades after the war, Japan had become the talk of the global town. In 1964, the year of the Beatles' first world tour, the New York Expo, and—of course—the Ford Mustang, Tokyo hosted the Summer Olympics. Japan carefully prepared for the event, staging a festival of technological creativity. But the showcased new photo finish cameras and the world's first satellite broadcasting system were thoroughly upstaged by the launch of the Tōkaidō Shinkansen. Exactly as planned, nine days before the opening of the games, the world's fastest train, with its iconic bullet nose, began connecting Tokyo and Osaka, at a steady 200 kph, in just four hours. Run with meticulous precision and an almost excessively formal sense of deference, which had the staff proudly saluting the trains entering the station, the Shinkansen turned out to have an enormous effect on the Japanese mobility habits: within three years, it had served 100 million passengers, and after twelve years, the one billion mark was exceeded. Long before the standard car could reach even remotely comparable top speeds, it was thus rendered useless for long distance commuting—also considering the speed limit on Japanese highways having been set, with the aim of enforcing safety, at a quite acceptable 100 kph. In general, it is fair to describe the Japanese relationship to speed as unique. For they may have had their Grand Prix and wide freeways—yet they never got to know the road movie, or the archetypical cool Le Mans hero for that matter. Culturally speaking, the country can appear immobile thanks to its strong protection of tradition—in the arts, handcrafts, lifestyle, and even the movies—against the interference of the outside world. Economically speaking, the society ran as fast as it could, quickly implementing new technologies, while simultaneously pushing, rather then following, the markets' pace. It seems as though business people were supposed to move fast as a group—aboard the Shinkansen—while the individual *sararīman* in his Bluebird or Corona was prompted to slowly and safely drive home. As if obliged to adopt the policy of *jishu-kisei*, or mutual self-restraint—the automobile industry accepted a

Mazda Cosmo Sport, 1967

maximum speed limit of 180 kph for all cars sold in the domestic market in the 1970s.

TECHNOMOTION

For the Japanese, technology has never been just a matter of sheer performance: eventually, it became some kind of feeling. When Akio Morita acquired the transistor technology from Western Electric, he concentrated on miniaturization. The result of his efforts, Sony's first pocketable radio of 1957, had no higher performance than other Western products. Instead, it was smaller—and personal, so to speak. Half a million units of this almost intimate piece of technology were sold within three years. And when the first 'direct view' portable TV followed in 1960, its exotic and expensive package made it the favorite of—to use Sony's words—the very rich and eccentric. With the launch of the Micro-TV and American customers raiding the brand's new Fifth Avenue showroom to buy it in 1962, Sony made the world change the way it looked at Japanese design. All of a sudden, products "Made in Japan" were perceived as hi-tech, hi-value goods. At home, after the Japanese family had struggled to acquire the essential "three sacred treasures" of the 1950s—television, refrigerator, and washing machine—interest was now converging towards more fashionable and enjoyable symbols of affluence. The must-have "three Cs" for 1965 were the cooler, the color TV set and, naturally, the car.

After it had traditionally only devoted a few lines of text to this emerging industry, the *Automobile Year* now suddenly dedicated a ten pages-long story to Japan in its 1962–63 issue, calling her "the third power in the world market." To prepare the story, director, Ami Guichard, and chief editor, Günther Molter, had undertaken a 26-hour flight on a Lufthansa Boeing 720B between

Sony TR-63, 1957

Sony Micro-TV, 1962

Shinkansen, 1964

Frankfurt and Tokyo—including stopovers at Rome, Cairo, Dharhan, Karachi, Calcutta, Bangkok, and Hong Kong. Their pictures of the 9th Tokyo Motor Show depict the newest car models, promoted by the inevitable female models. In order to underline the global ambitions, their dress code was rarely Japanese. So even if Toyota stuck to the kimono for the Toyopet Crown Deluxe, Nissan actually preferred a sleek Western evening dress with a fur gown for its Cedric Special, whereas the Subaru 360—still described as "classical" in its design—even dared exhibiting a leg-long black fishnet pantyhose on high heels. In comparison, the girl sitting inside the silver Toyota Publica Sports prototype was almost underdressed in some kind of sporty sweater. Apart from that, the small aerodynamic sports car with its jet fighter style sliding roof looked too concept car-like to have any chance of ever becoming a reality. But three years later, an enthusiastic Japanese public could finally buy a sports car of Japanese breed: the Toyota 800 Sports. Its eye-catching lightweight body may not have been too refined in its details—that is, except for its oversized headlamps with molded fairings and their thick, manga style chrome rings. And, with kind regards to Porsche, Toyota's baby racer also sported the world's first series production removable Targa roof. On the next page of *Automobile Year*, two little cars appeared that did not seem to require female company: the new Honda Sports models—a silver S360 and a red S500 roadster of utterly modern, low and sleek style—which the European editors agreed to call the "sensation of the motor show." Having dominated the Isle of Man TT races, Honda itself had actually been the sensation of the sixties. In some ways, this company, founded and led by Soichiro Honda, reflected the rebellious spirit of Sony. The consumer electronics sensation, then named Totsuko, had actually entered the

Toyota Publica Sports, 1962

Honda S500, 1963

Honda RA 273, 1966

radio business against all warnings and, in 1958, contrary to the advice of the mighty Mitsui Bank, even dared change its brand name into the *gaijin*—foreign-sounding Sony. In similar spirit, Honda had entered the automotive business by openly opposing MITI orders, thus bringing the winning technology of its motorbikes to the car sector. Honda's compact, lightweight four cylinder engines could rev as high as 9,500 rpm and beyond, delivering twice as much power as any competitor's. Besides, two months before the Tokyo Olympics would start, Honda had impressed the world's sports scene by starting at the German Grand Prix at the Nürburgring with a works Formula 1 car—which, in its ivory white livery, with a red sun dot on top, was a wonderfully iconic symbol of the Japanese technological sunrise.

SPECIALS

The film industry just could not wait to jump on the new bandwagon. As MGM was preparing its *Grand Prix* movie, featuring the Honda F1 team, Columbia Pictures readied *Walk, Don't Run*, set during the Tokyo Olympics and starring Cary Grant in his last feature film. These two 1966 movie highlights were good enough reason for the famed duo of producers, Broccoli and Saltzman, to film their next James Bond adventure, *You Only Live Twice*, in Japan. Apart from the rather implausible disguise of Sean Connery as a Japanese fisherman, the movie's highlight must be the mysteriously beautiful Toyota 2000 GT. This Gran Turismo of classic European stature—meaning the long bonnet and short tail of a Jaguar E-Type—is often said to be based on a concept that German-American designer, Albrecht Count Goertz, had penned on behalf of Yamaha, who

Toyota 2000 GT, 1965

later built the 2000 GT for Toyota. But that car's designer had in fact been Japanese and his name was never officially released. When presenting the 2000 GT, the first car of Japanese origin to receive such treatment, *Automobile Quarterly* called it an "outstanding high performance (...) superlative machine." The prestigious magazine's article began with a rather unusual foreword: "The following article was prepared for *AQ* by the designer of the Toyota 2000 GT. It is a policy of the Toyota company that individual credit may not be given to any member of their design staff, as all products are considered to be fruit of the Toyota family efforts. Though we would be pleased to do so, we must naturally honor Toyota's request, and omit the writer's name." Today, rumor has it that the mystery designer's name was Satoru Nozaki, about whom not much is known. Nozaki's article contains much of the theory behind the design—a progressive external shape, coupled with a conservative ambience for the interior—and its development, explaining the car's style down to the smallest details, such as the molding around the lamps, which the designer was not satisfied with. And indeed, while the car is an unquestionably beautiful shape and was up to date when it was announced in 1965, it was no longer particularly progressive once it went on sale in 1967—the year, lest we forget, of Bertone's Marzal. Judged against its contemporaries, one notices how innovative elements, such as the molded metal tail-lights' encasing—which anticipated a certain fashion by some 40 years—mingle with features inspired by Italian designs of the period, among them the 1962 Fiat Abarth by Pininfarina or the 1963 Lamborghini by Franco Scaglione—who that same year also penned the Prince Skyline 1900 Sprint. Equally exotic was the Datsun Coupé 1500, first unveiled in 1964 and about to enter handmade production as the Nissan Silvia in 1965. Possibly

Mazda Cosmo, 1964

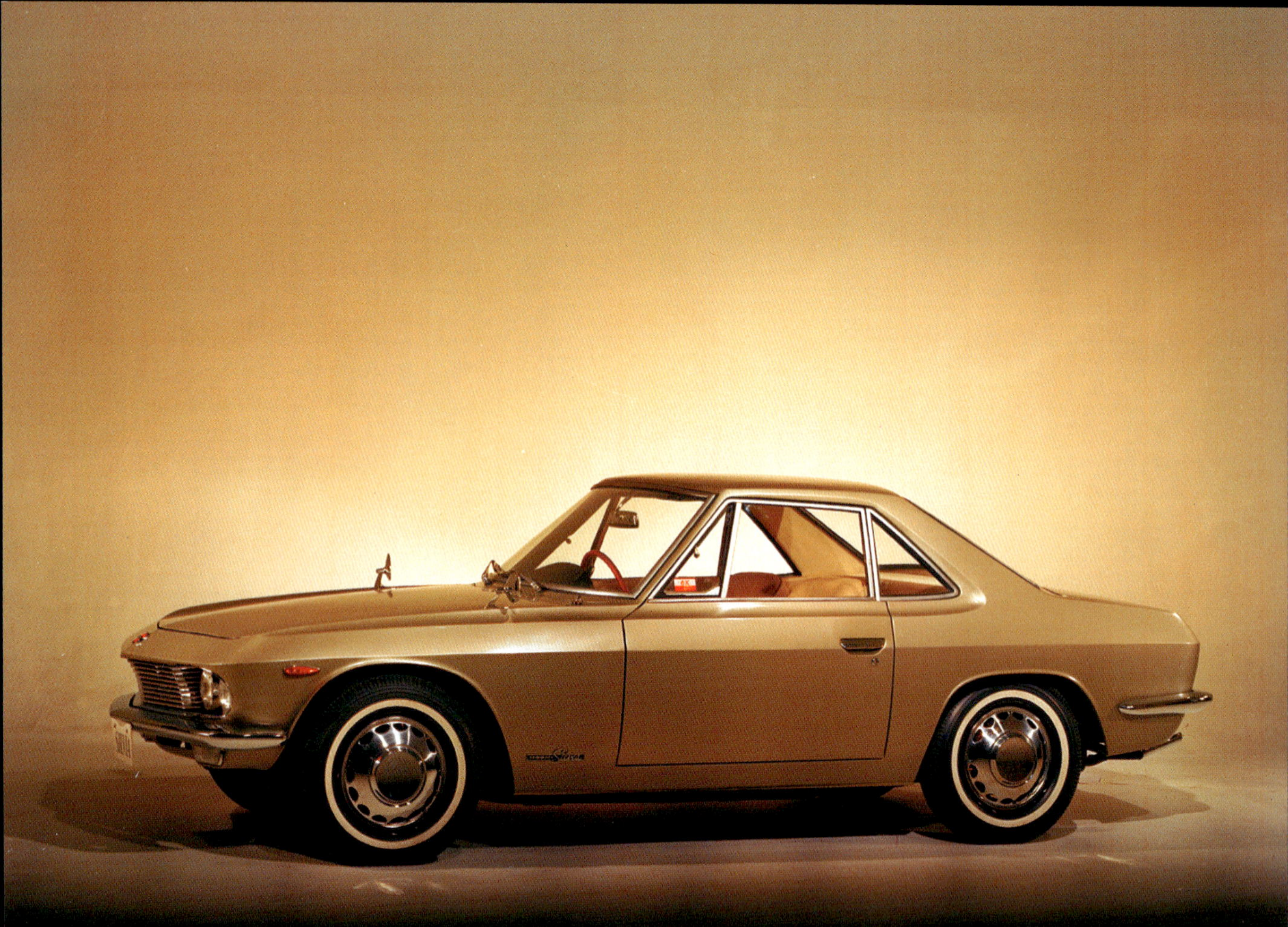

designed in collaboration with the seemingly ubiquitous Count Goertz, this was a car of enchanting elegance, anticipating, in terms of packaging and style, the Queen of Montecarlo Lancia Fulvia Coupé—to which, had it been made available to Europe, it would have posed as a much sharper alternative.

As if by coincidence, turning a few pages of the very same No. 10 Japanese feature issue of *Automobile Year*, the technology-savvy reader could delve into a critical revue of the much-discussed rotary engine, as developed by Felix Wankel for NSU of Germany. After having pointed out a great many weaknesses, the editors maintained a good degree of skepticism regarding its possible realization on an industrial scale. They seemed to have ignored that at the same time, Toyo Kogyo had already knocked on the Germans' door and was now granted first rights to exploit the new technology. By 1963, the Wankel-powered Mazda Cosmo Sport prototype was up and running. This was an evocative design concept, a lightweight streamline shape, akin to a late homage to the imaginative "superflow" rocket design, as seen in Italy and the US during the 1950s, but—if one was inclined to see it that way—also anticipating yet to come bestsellers like the 1966 Alfa Romeo Spider. In 1967, Mazda was finally ready to put the rotary Cosmo in production.

Compared to the overall output of the industry—10 million between 1965 and 1970—all these specials were a most marginal business: just 351 of the big sports Toyota were made and even of the smaller one only a meager 3,500 examples. The Silvia stopped at 500, the Cosmo at 1,500 units. Mostly reserved to Japan, these designs were simply not globally visible enough to cause much of a stir. But thanks to a strong sex-appeal-to-economy-ratio and clear focus on the export markets, Honda meanwhile sold at least 25,000

Datsun Fairlady, 1963

roadsters and coupés of the types S500, 600, and 800 over the course of eight years. Sales figures could not measure the halo effect though: highlighting technology rather than performance, the Japanese brands quickly upgraded their former rugged, no-frills image. They were about to surf the American wave of Pony and Muscle Cars, challenge the original British roadster and the practical German sports car, or simply pioneer new niches—with the market eagerly following. Originating from the 1960–75 design euphoria were such highlights as the Nissan Skyline GT-R, the Isuzu Bellet GT or the Datsun Fairlady SP310 roadster. What many consider a copy of the more successful MGB was in fact presented at the very same time. One should not forget though that MG belonged to the same British Motors Corporation that in turn owned Austin, a company with which Nissan had established intense relations. Demonstrating advanced marketing skills, to promote the car during the Summer Olympics, Nissan established a showroom inside the Ginza department store, the cradle of fashion in downtown Tokyo, and engaged a group of female hostesses, obviously called Miss Fairlady.

Of a similar nature was the Isuzu 117 Coupé of 1966, a fastback designed by Giorgetto Giugiaro. Not only as good-looking as the Fiat Dino Coupé—also penned by Giugiaro—the 117 was also one of the first Japanese cars equipped with a DOHC engine, the very first with fuel injection and the world's first sports car also available with a diesel engine. With a production run of roughly 50,000 and 90,000 units respectively, supported by steady demand from the US, the Datsun roadster and the Isuzu coupé paved the American way for the first really big thing coming from Japan: the 1969 Datsun Fairlady 240 Z. Designed between 1965 and '68 as a modern, yet classical fastback Berlinetta by Yoshihiko Matsuo (head of

Datsun Fairlady Z 432, 1971

Datsun Bluebird SSS, 1968

EXPO, Osaka, 1970

Design Studio #4 at Nissan), engineered to challenge Porsche, marketed in a variety of more or less sporty configurations, the exotic but affordable "Z" became an instant bestseller in God's Own Country and was bound to become the world's most successful sports car. Upon its launch, the flowing Z-line with the classically encapsulated round headlights was actually just about to appear old-fashioned by European standards—where the spunky car consequentially sold quite poorly. Still, one look at this Fairlady should suffice to understand the raison d'être of Porsche's front-engined 924–944 sports cars of the 1970s.

SPEED SUSHI

Heading towards 1970, the Japanese attention to design had grown and was now emancipated to a point where it could venture into iconic and experimental territory—the results extending from the black square of Sony's Trinitron, the world's best color TV, to the plated gold of Seiko's Astron, the world's first quartz watch. Among radios alone, one had the choice of either the smart cube of Sony's TR-1825 or the pop sphere of National Panasonic's Panapet. Both were released for the World's Fair at Osaka, itself a festival of the experimental, masterminded by Kenzo Tange, mixing hi-tech pagodas, inflatable structures and electronic pavilions. Its 65 million visitors within six months prove the scale of the global attention the Expo '70 received—a record that was only surpassed by Shanghai in 2010. Considering the copious scale of this design ferment, it could only ever have been a matter of time before this exoticism would reach the *kei* car segment. And as if to give Nissan a healthy kick in the backside, Honda duly launched its own Z-design in 1970. This sports coupé version of Honda's N-series city car featured sinuous lines, with a low, Fairlady-like

Sony Trinitron, 1968

Sony TR-1825, 1970

Honda Z GS, 1971

nose and a sharp Kamm tail, itself marked by a characteristic matte black tailgate. As if this were not enough, the little Honda was also shown with a hardtop-style roof and a very rebellious matte body finish. In 1971, Suzuki marched on with the Fronte Coupé. The edgy, just slightly wedge-lined "Japanese Miura" was effectively advertised as a "two seater coupé for lovers." What Z was to Nissan and Honda, RX was to Mazda. In contrast to European received wisdom—inextricably linked to the ill-famed NSU Ro80—the Japanese actually succeeded in making and marketing a whole range of exotic rotary-engined cars, starting with the 1969 Familia Rotary SS. Albeit hardly for their "innocuously styled" mainstream design, the RX-2 Capella, RX-3 Savanna, RX-4 Luce, and RX-5 Cosmo were warmly welcomed due to their captivating rotary performance, and sold in hundreds of thousands—at least before the oil crisis hit Mazda. But even after this shock, and a perilous shift back to combustion engines, Mazda remained faithful to its rotary and, in 1978, launched the pretty RX-7. With its no-nonsense pop-up headlights and the glazed rear panorama dome, it was less an exotikar, than a product specifically designed to attack the four cylinder Porsches on the US market. With a price advantage of roughly 50%, the first generation RX-7 alone eventually outsold the 924–944 range by 1:5. The last, but not least 1970s novelty was less exotic in style than packaging. Iconic and innovative off-road vehicles had by then become a Japanese staple: shortly before the Toyota Hi-Lux pickup popped up in 1968, the already legendary Land Cruiser spawned the big and classic "iron pig" station wagon, while Suzuki miniaturized the original version into the 1969 Jimny. The Subaru Leone 4WD then went about combining jeep-like traction, station wagon loading capacity and sedan ride quality in 1972, outlining a

National Panasonic R70, 1970

Mazda Savanna RX-7, 1978

new market niche, catering to the affluent leisure society. In Europe, "the Subaru" became the choice for the urban upper bourgeoisie, who, at the weekend, would head for their alpine chalets for winter sports and *après ski*. Then head of research and development at Audi, Ferdinand Piëch, a passionate skier himself, must have spotted quite a few of them, before finally deciding to go on his own Quattro project.

Sports cars and roadsters may have played a minor role in the Japanese market, where even today they constitute a rather rare occurrence: of the first million Datsun Zs produced, more than 80% were exported. Yet for some reason beyond what could otherwise be called self-indulgence, the Japanese carmakers' passion for the exotic never quite faded away. The Mazda RX, the Honda S, the Nissan Z, and the Toyota GT may have come and gone—but, as history has shown, it was never too late for a comeback. Just after Honda had stopped stimulating the public with the very exotic S2000 roadster—a little S500 on anabolic steroids—of which about 100,000 were produced over 10 years time, Lexus proposed the limited edition LFA super sports car, which many considered a tribute to the original Toyota 2000 GT. So, no matter how distant the charms of the '60s may appear, Japan actually never stopped loving the Fair Lady since.

Subaru Leone 4WD Station Wagon, 1972

Toyota Hi-Lux, 1968

Suzuki Jimny, 1970

Mazda Cosmo Sport, 1970

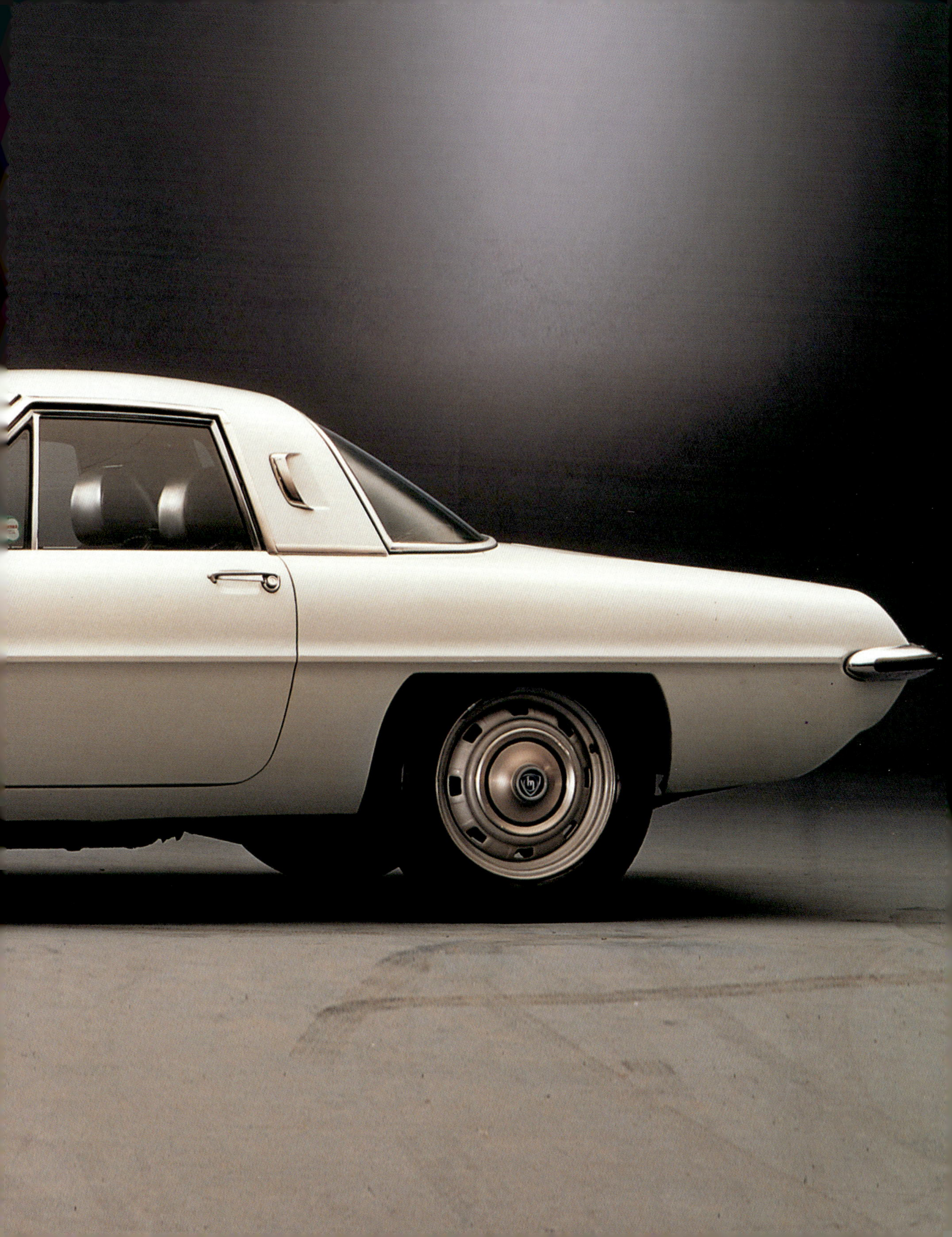

Honda S500, 1963

Honda S800 Coupé, 1966

Toyota Sports 800, 1965

Toyota 2000 GT, 1965

YAMAHA

That the 2000 GT became a legend is more often attributed to mother Toyota than to its almost unknown father. In the mid-1960s, Yamaha, the engineering company and motorcycle producer, considered entering the automotive industry. As collaboration among peers has never been an issue in Japan, a joint venture was planned with Nissan, with the aim of creating what could have become the Z sports car. But once things did not work out as intended, Yamaha knocked on Toyota's door instead. Not in spite of its image as the most conservative Japanese car brand, but because of it and to thus counteract it, Toyota agreed to give birth to Japan's first supercar which was, in fact, skillfully built in a hi-tech manufacturing department by Yamaha.

Isuzu 117 Coupé, 1966

Isuzu Bellett GT-R, 1973

ISUZU

Hard to spot amidst all the diesel trucks and utility vehicles, Isuzu does have a rich history of passenger cars. Back in the 1960s, it was one of Japan's Big Three! Its first passenger car to leave a mark was the pretty 117 Coupé, styled by then chief designer of Ghia, Giorgetto Giugiaro. The 117's mainstream cousin, the Bellett, spawned a racy GT-R variant, featuring not only enhanced performance, but also styling tweaks like the crucial black bonnet, which set trends among the Japanese car racing community. In keeping with Isuzu's underdog fortunes, the GT-R moniker only reached greater fame once employed by others. With the 117 Coupé somewhat past its prime after 13 years in production, the task was once again given to Giugiaro to come up with a successor. The Italian duly delivered with the cutting-edge Piazza coupé in 1980, whose futuristic looks—inside and out—did their utmost to distract from its fairly outdated underpinnings. Unfortunately, sharp coupés alone could not prevent Isuzu from quite a few identity crises, most notably during the unstable, decades-long cooperation with General Motors. Today, the brand remains big in heritage—or in new trucks.

Nissan Skyline GT-R, 1969

Nissan R381, 1968

Nissan Skyline GT-R, 1969

SHINICHIRO SAKURAI

Here we have perhaps the most outstanding of Japanese automotive engineers. Trained at Nakajima Hikoki aircraft manufacturers after the Second World War, Shinichiro Sakurai was hired by the Prince Motor Co. to design the Skyline, whose breed—which could be described as a Japanese Alfa Romeo Giulia—is, to all intents and purposes, his baby. Developed into the racing pop star GT-R, his S54 2 liter Skyline famously chased a Porsche 904 GTS during the 1964 Japan GP. This experience led to Sakurai's conjuring of the Prince R380 mid-engined race car—which finally won the 1966 GP at Fuji Speedway, ahead of Porsche. When Nissan absorbed Prince, Mr. Skyline followed suit, bringing both the Skyline and a racing heritage with him, both of which he kept up and running until 2011—when he passed away, aged 81 and still in charge of Nissan's specialist car division, Autech.

YUTAKA KATAYAMA

A quintessential car guy, Yutaka Katayama was to Nissan what importer Max Hoffman was to the German car industry. Instrumental in establishing Datsun on the US market during the 1960s and '70s, he, unlike many of his Japanese peers, not only loved the product he was selling, but he was also fond of the market he was selling it to. That enabled him to understand the Americans and what they desired in a car—which was not only a bit of fun to go with all that reliability and good value, but also bigger engines and certainly not silly names like Fairlady or Bluebird. Katayama—or Mr. K, as he was soon rechristened in all-American fashion by his *gaijin* peers—therefore fought for the Bluebird 510 and its powerful engine and against the flowery Fairlady badge on a promising new small sports car. His solution was to simply call it by its internal code: the number 240, followed by the sexy letter Z.

Nissan Fairlady 240ZG, 1971

Nissan Fairlady 240ZG, 1971

Nissan Fairlady 240Z, East African Safari Rally, 1973

Ikonik 118

Nissan 260Z 2+2, 1974

Nissan 280Z, 1975

Nissan 280Z 2+2, 1975

Yoshio Nakamura and Soichiro Honda, Honda RA 273, 1966

Honda Z, 1970

SOICHIRO HONDA

Adventurer. Non-conformist. Maverick. Hardly the characterizations typically associated with Japanese industrialists, but Soichiro Honda was all of the above, and more. Along with Sony's Akio Morita, he is the ultimate Japanese entrepreneur, and the one and only mythical figure of Japanese motoring history—someone who stands with his head held high amidst the Enzo Ferraris and Ferdinand Porsches. During the pursuit of his love of all things engineering, Mr. Honda created what would become Japan's biggest producer of motorcycles, before turning his attention towards automobiles. The almighty MITI did not take kindly to Honda's ambitions, but Honda created a *fait accompli* in the tiny shape of the S500 roadster, which proved that there actually were niches of the car market hitherto unserved. This was only a small beginning for Honda's automotive ambitions, but over the years success in motor racing—a passion of his—and strong sales, particularly in the US—a market whose can-do attitude Honda always felt close to—cemented his legacy. As the original ads for the Cub motorcycle said: "you meet the nicest people on a Honda." Soichiro surely was one of those.

Honda Z Hard Top, 1973

Subaru R-2 SS, 1970

Suzuki Jimny 8, 1970

Suzuki Fronte Coupé GE, 1971

WASABI KEI

Having rebuilt his economy in record time over the two decades in the Second World War's aftermath, the Japanese car driver could finally grant himself a bit of escapism. Not too much of it, mind you, but something that exuded some exotic appeal: a tiny bit of spicy raciness within the *kei* car's strict confines would be nice. This desire was satisfied from 1970 onwards, when the Suzuki Fronte Coupé, nicknamed the "Japanese Miura", the Honda Z, more of a saucy tomboy than a Fairlady Z and the Subaru R-2 SS offered a whiff of coupé decadence on a microscale. Suzuki's Jimny even opened up the wide world of off-roading to decent *kei* car owners. Finally, there was wasabi spice lurking in even the tiniest of cars.

Subaru Leone, 1972

Toyota Hi-Lux 4WD, 1979

Toyota Land Cruiser J5 "iron pig", 1967

Mazda Capella RE Coupé, 1971

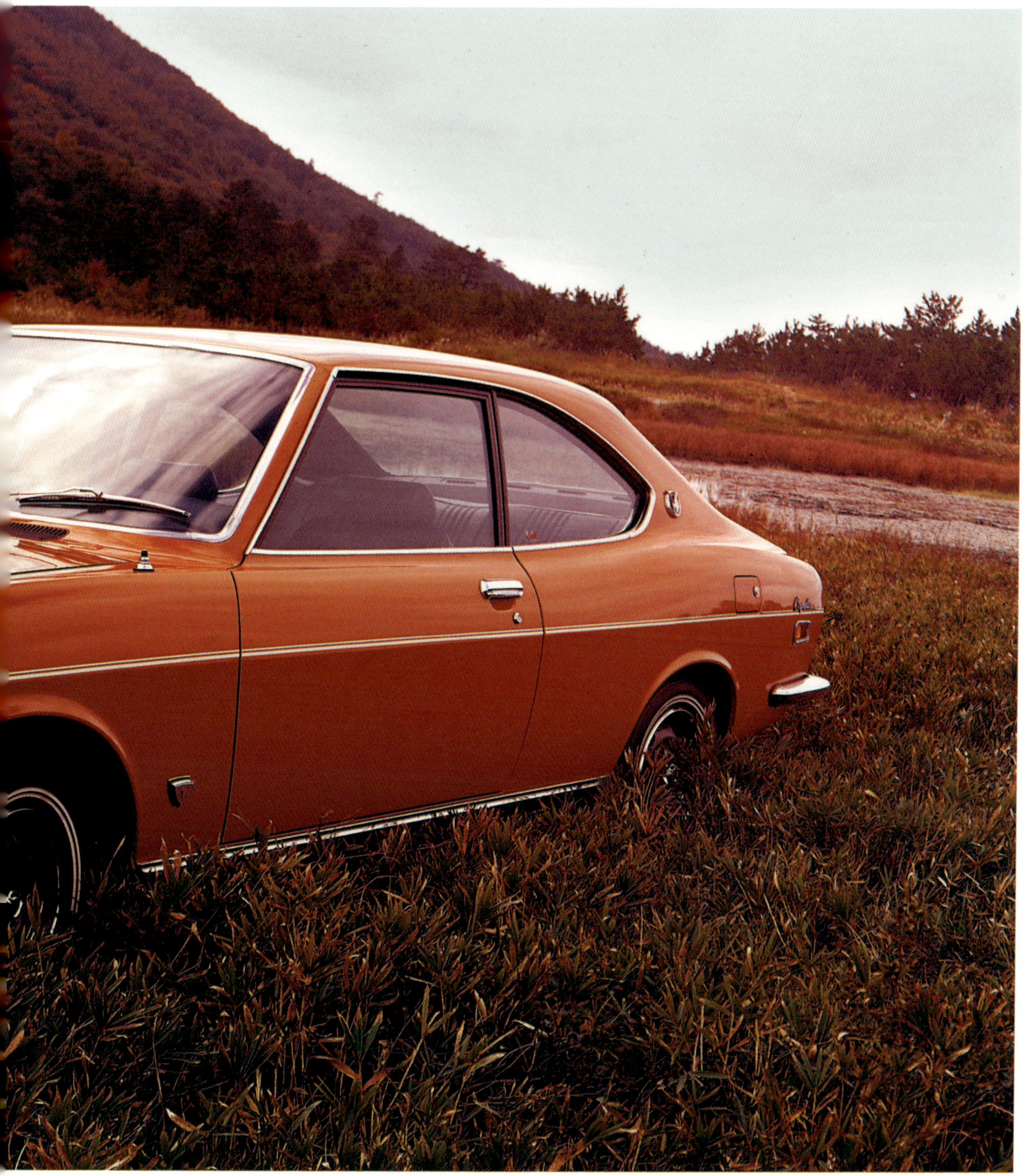

Mazda Luce Rotary Coupé, 1969

Mazda Cosmo AP, 1975

TSUNEJI MATSUDA

Adopted son of the founder of Toyo Kogyo, and later to become president of Mazda, Tsuneji Matsuda succeeded where the might of German engineers failed. Because of his visions, he was often referred to as "the Soichiro Honda of West Japan." Matsuda believed in the rotary engine by Felix Wankel as a means of establishing Mazda's leadership in the industry. Yet what Matsuda and chief engineer, Kenichi Yamamoto, really were after was paying tribute to the victims of the atomic bombs, the consequences of which they both had been personally confronted with. In a Herculean effort, the two of them turned Mazda's RE—for Rotary Engined—and the RX sports cars into a success. Their combination of exotic engineering and distinguished style enchanted the US market and helped sharpening up Mazda's image, right until air pollution CAFE regulations got in the way. Sales fell from almost 200,000 in 1972 to less then half of that one year later. But by then, the capabilities of the Hiroshima-based company were beyond reproach. Just as it had survived the bomb, Matsuda's company survived the crisis—and the rotary engines got to live on until today.

Nissan Silvia, 1975

Nissan Silvia, 1975

Mazda Savanna RX-7, 1978

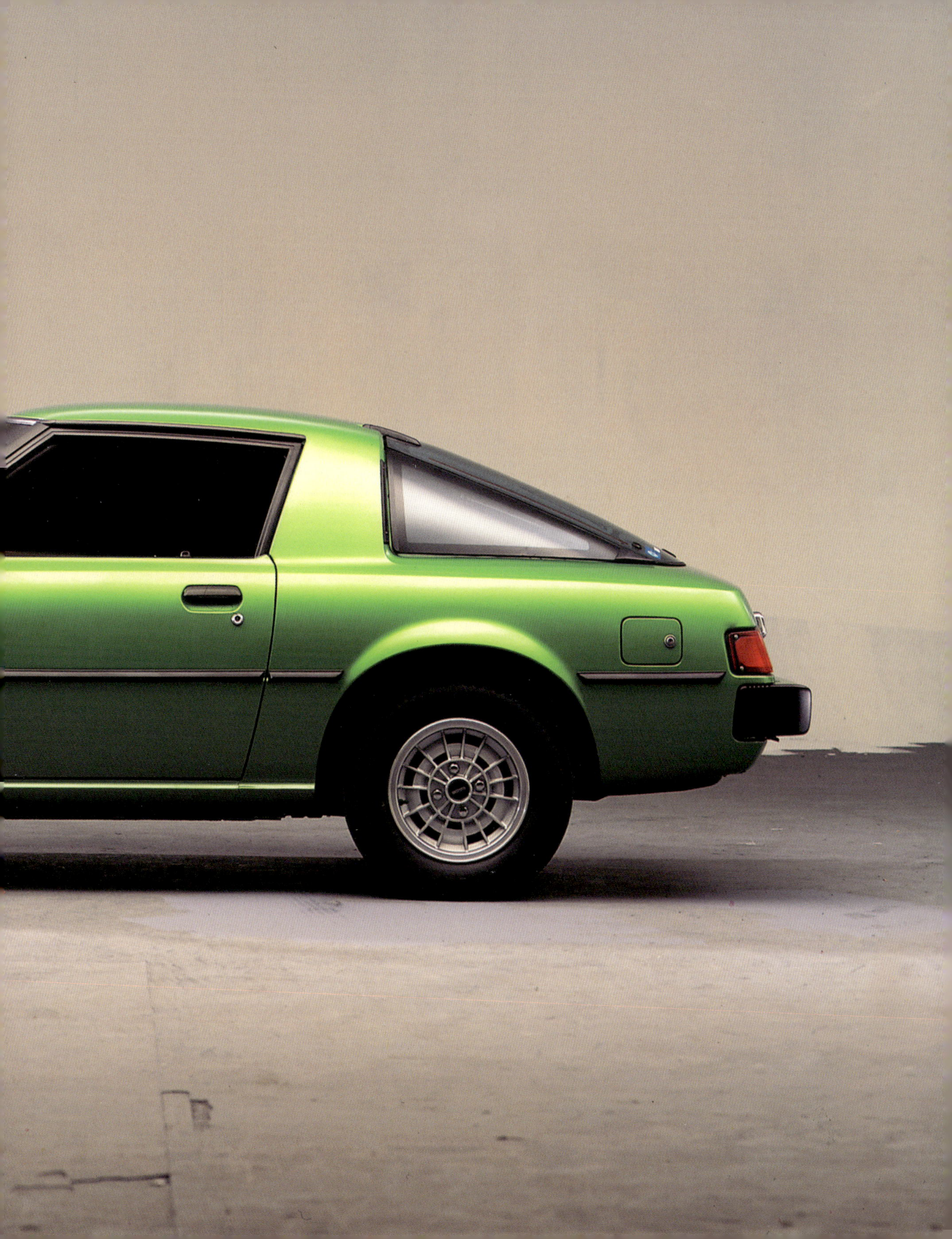

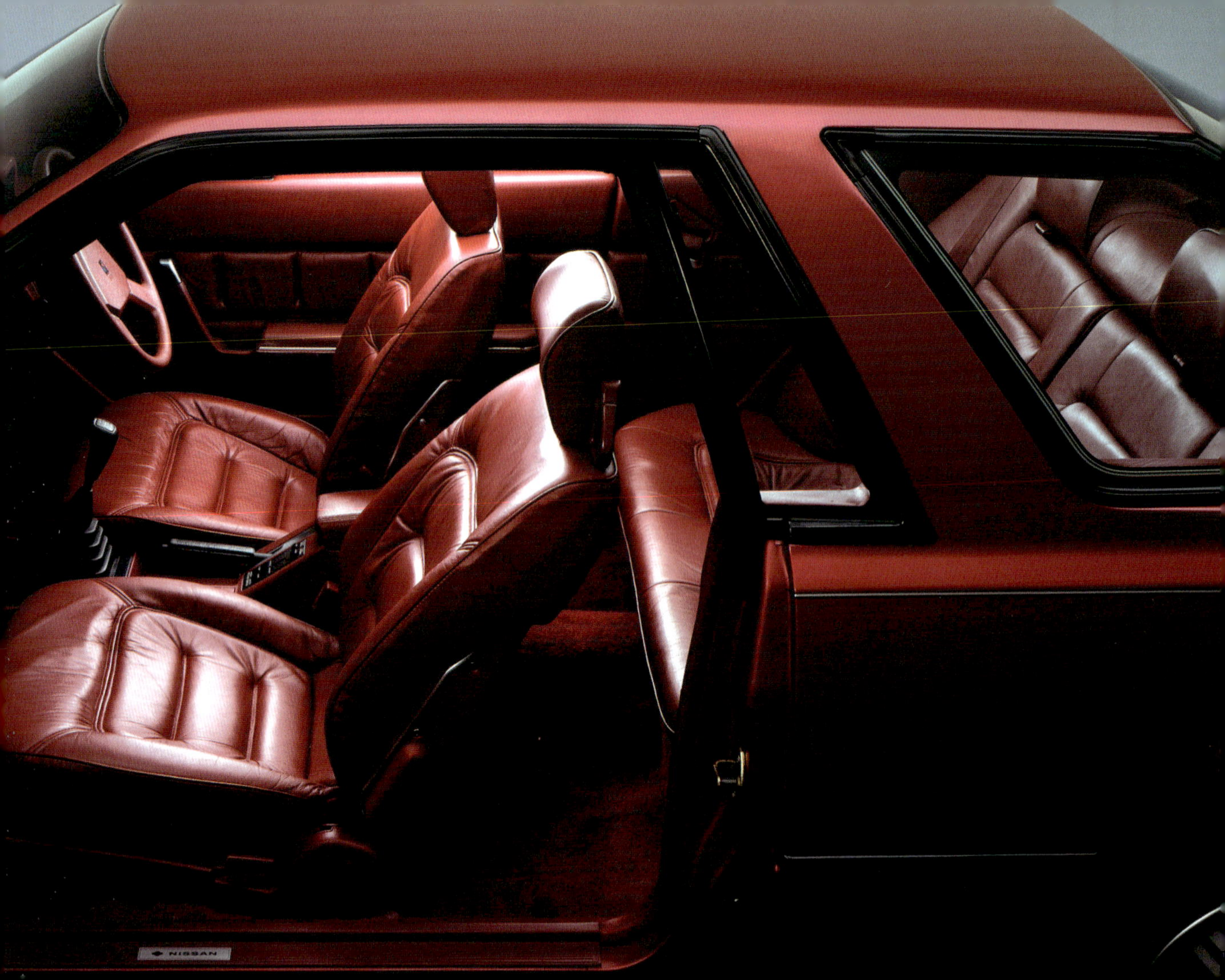
NISSAN

FULL FLAT

If the fifties had been adventurous, the sixties challenging, and the seventies successful, then the Japanese eighties were simply magic. Since 1970, the economy had been growing at a steady 4% and wages on average at 6% every year. As a result, the Japanese had more than doubled their share in the world household consumption expenditures by 1986 and were spending ten times as much money as they had fifteen years earlier.

Cars ranked high on the list of nice things to have: at the end of the eighties, there were thirty million of them around—three times as many as in 1970—and the industry was producing around 10 million new ones every year. As if to prove that Japan had become a leader not only in number and quality, but also in performance, Honda even went back to Formula 1 in 1983. And this time it was to win—which it did, and to great applause, too: both with and without turbo, earning six world champion constructor's titles in a row, first with Williams, then with McLaren. Supercharged by this financial and industrial performance, Japanese culture was inevitably changing, and so was the image of the country. Every yuppie around Manhattan now had to speak Japanese, while Daryl Hannah and Charlie Sheen turned sushi into the yuppiest food of them all in Oliver Stone's movie *Wall Street*. In France, the aesthetic principles of Japanese food had already influenced Paul Bocuse's nouvelle cuisine. Spearheaded by *maki* and *nigiri*, Japan's post-modern avant-garde had arrived in its entirety. In fashion, the 1980s brought about Yōji Yamamoto's streetwear chic, established Rei Kawakubo's Comme des Garçons in Paris and introduced Issey Miyake's experimental pleats—all of them demonstrating a new Japanese *Weltanschauung*. And CoSTUME NATIONAL, founded in 1986 and, despite sounding Parisian, actually a Milanese brand, was led by an Italian designer who had learnt the job at Yamamoto's studio. In architecture, the old master, Kenzō Tange, won the Pritzker Architecture Prize, while the highly aesthetic brutalism of his dotted, naked concrete was making the designs of Tadao Ando world famous—the consequence being that Ando got his Pritzker too. Just like a

Nissan Leopard 280X hardtop coupé, 1980

kimono shell, Ando's spiritual minimalism concealed an essence of the same hi-tech that was leading the way in consumer electronics. In this sector, Pioneer had pioneered a new design philosophy in the hi-fi business, pushing forward a fascinating manifestation of technology that materialized in enchanting spectroscopic displays and culminated in the totemic hi-fi rack—the new status symbol of the discerning 1980s household. Casio's C-80 calculator watch reflects the same hi-tech look, its matte black block featuring more buttons than one would ever hope to control through "fingertip operation." When the simply iconic, lifestyle-changing Sony Walkman appeared in 1979, one could feel as though Japan was finally delivering all the things one had always dreamt of—but had been afraid to ask for.

Technology became the mother language of a new stage in Japanese car design. Contributing to this change had been a shift of interest towards Europe. The old and fragmented market, characterized by strong protectionism and high cultural barriers, had initially been no priority for the Japanese manufacturers—until 1970, export to Europe had therefore been utterly irrelevant. In a similar vein, the Japanese had always appreciated the European automobile's design, yet never quite wanted or needed to reach the same level of sophistication. In a kind of transitional phase, Mazda had started to promote a sleeker, more international and less baroque styling over the course of the 1970s. The middle class 626 and the new 'Great Little Car', the 323 for 1976, both had rear wheel drive, like in the olden days—and like the new-for-1978 Toyota Starlet. Following a boxy new Galant for 1976, Mitsubishi's front wheel drive Colt turned out to be the most European of them all, in terms of style and feel. But the two oil crises during the seventies proved the superiority of the European approach, with innovative

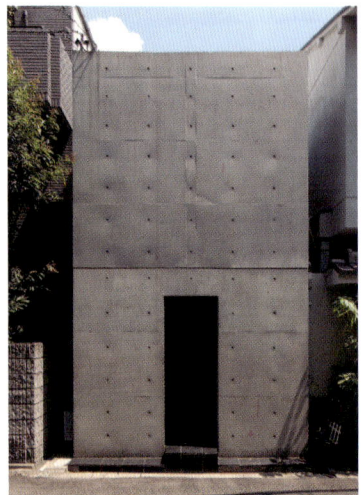

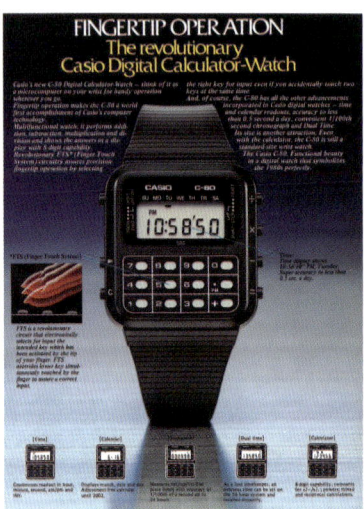

Azuma House, Tadao Ando, Osaka, 1976   Casio C-80, 1980   Pioneer hi-end rack, 1980

cars that were smaller and smarter, as well as more stylish then all the others. As Japan was growing and the American model was losing ground, the Europeans therefore kept their share of the global business. And not only were they making twice as many passenger cars as the Japanese—their cars were also perceived as being more valuable, too. This was reflected in the figures: The European share of the US market compared to the Japanese was only 30% of its volume, but 54% of its dollar value. The European edge design of the '70 and '80s, coupled with sophisticated technology, was worth some 80% more to US customers than Japanese-American design.

FLATS PLEASE

Despite having had first-hand experience with European manufacturers, and repeated cooperation with the Italian car design consultancies, it was actually Akira Fujimoto's influential quarterly magazine, *Car Styling*, that, new for 1973, finally put Japanese car design page-to-page with the Italian cutting edge—and, to a lesser degree—wedge design. The innovative, radical Italian approach to car design seemed to be the perfect match to the flatness of tatami mats and *shōji* walls, the solid geometry of sashimi or the Trinitron. Although to this day many may find it hard to appreciate, following the intrinsic rational logic and emotional subtlety of 1980s style, Japanese design was finally able to reveal its unique aesthetic quality. With flatness as a motivational principle of Japanese arts, car design was now in a position to stretch this to its maximum extent. Inevitably, some of the results of this development were just too flat, or too angular, or too thin. The proportions were not always ideal, and nor was all the surface modelling faultless. A masterpiece à la Pininfarina is hard to find, yet conversely—

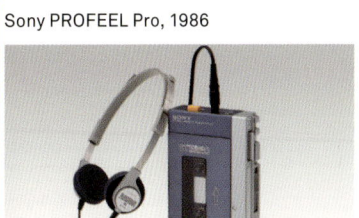

Nissan CUE-X, 1985

Sony PROFEEL Pro, 1986

Sony Walkman, 1979

and in a very Japanese way—the creative standard was of a very high level. By going flat, the Japanese car finally gained independence from its squeezed look, gained a wide body, and with it a wholly new self-confidence. Within this context, it should not be forgotten that during this same period of time, the Americans had begun downsizing their cathedrals into new baroque cabins, while the Europeans—save for, perhaps, some Germans—were treating their '70s designs to some black plastic cosmetics. Behind the Japanese flatness, deep hi-tech detailing emerged, which would be seen in the bold graphic underline, the crisp treatment of surfaces and in complex structural solutions. As was '80s fashion, the body was tattooed with digital displays, control panels, and the inevitable masses of stickers and badges to advertise the technology underneath the skin, as Nissan introduced the Turbo in the 1979 Cedric, Honda pioneered 4WS—four wheel steering—in the 1987 Prelude and Mitsubishi put 5 valves per cylinder into its Dangan ZZ in 1989. The odd Western performance badge made its appearance on the massive Debonair by AMG, the zippy Daihatsu Charade by De Tomaso or the Nissan Pulsar Milano X1 powered by Alfa Romeo: clearly, in post-modern times, all this—style and technology—was but a reinvention of the wheel. Yet the Japanese series of cars of the '80s was not simply copying the Europeans, it was justifiably leading the show. In order to achieve this feat, the flexibility of Japanese manufacturing systems had been employed to afford the creative freedom that the Europeans and Americans—who had both been hit hard by the deep crises during the '70s—could not afford anymore. Meanwhile in the Far East, not only the hardtop limousine, but the coupé and the limited production bodies had survived. Having the money to invest, the Japanese were now the first to elaborate on

Mitsubishi Debonair AMG, 1989

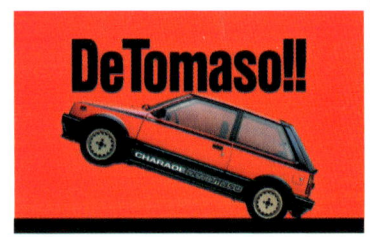

Daihatsu Charade De Tomaso Turbo, 1983   Italdesign Megagamma, 1978

innovative concepts and to risk challenges. They were safe in the knowledge that in design, no risk is bound to equal no fun.

TALL PLEASE

Few concept cars have been more influential and less appreciated than the Italdesign Megagamma. This prototype of the intelligent tall car, shown by Giugiaro at the Turin Automobile Show in 1978, had all the virtues but one: sex appeal. Fiat deemed the Lancia badged "maxi Golf" simply too risky to put into production—and that was the end of the story. But on the other side of the world, someone got the message. And so, after a pregnancy of merely three years—so short was the time the Japanese needed to do an all-new car from scratch—the Nissan Prairie was born: a tall, boxy, seven-seater with pillarless construction and rear sliding doors. In terms of concept and packaging, it was pure Megagamma; in terms of design and style, it was a car of its own. It also had a smaller sibling in the racy Honda City of the same year and with a similar concept. The Japanese reinvented the Mini by lending the cramped compactness of the original the Megagamma's height advantage. This really was the car British Leyland ought to have done instead of the 1980 Mini Metro.

The City-line originated from its smiling round eyes, went along a sloping wedge bonnet, ending in a wide, tall box of enchanting comfort and utmost practicality. Four body styles were available: hatchback, van, convertible, and high-roof. Besides innumerable trim levels, Honda also offered the Motocompo mobility option—a compact motorbike, designed to fit the style and space of the car. So even if they did not devise the concept, the Japanese unquestionably created and spread the "Tall Boy" trend.

Nissan Prairie, 1981

Honda City, 1981

Honda Motocompo, 1981

Toyota Sprinter Trueno 3door „AE 86" *hachi-roku*, 1983

The City may have been Giugiaro-inspired, but the creative minds behind Honda's second generation Prelude were the virtuosos of Pininfarina, the master design consultancy. Leonardo Fioravanti, former design director, recalls how new designs were imagined and modelled in Turin and then sent to Hamamatsu, in order to serve as a reference for the local designers. It was Soichiro Honda's wish (or order) that nothing should simply be copied. Instead, every model had to be redone in-house, with the intention to learn on the one side and evolve the homegrown skills on the other. According to Fioravanti, "none of Pininfarina's concepts were produced unchanged, but here and there you would find many of our solutions and, overall, recognize the guidelines that gave Honda a very distinctive face in the 1980s." And not just among Japanese competitors, but also as a reference among competitors worldwide. So, from 1982 onwards, the sleek Prelude bestowed a sporty face and a sharper edge upon the Honda brand, affecting the development of the later Accord, including Aerodeck, and Vigor. The latter featured not only the characteristic pop-up headlights—which perfectly matched the low bonnet made possible by a sophisticated suspension system—but also a unique glass tailgate distinctively cut into the rooftop. A similar body style characterized the third generation Civic for 1983, which anticipated the eye-catching black look tail, later to be seen on the Lancia Y10. After this iconic hatchback, and alongside a sedan, the panoramic Civic Shuttle was launched, a crossover between van and miniwagon. Most risky of them all, however, was Honda's Ballade Sports CR-X—the Japanese Car of the Year for 1984—which was released just at a time when all manufacturers and many customers were mourning the sports car's death. *Automobile Quarterly* spotted a visual resemblance "to an uncanny degree" to the

Honda Civic Shuttle, 1983

Honda Civic, 1983

Honda Ballade Sports CR-X Si, 1984

old Alfa Romeo Junior Zagato. Here was a car that was sporty outside and great inside, with the most practical of all 2+2-seat configurations and beautiful overall detailing—including pop-up headlights, available on selected trim levels. At the technological front, lightweight construction and good aerodynamics, coupled with Honda's electronic engine management, made for the impossible: top performance, high fuel efficiency, and lowest emissions, all at once. It was, in all Japanese modesty, a gem.

The Japanese went about reviving the market for off-road vehicles in similar fashion. Toyota further revamped the Land Cruiser lineup with the now legendary J7 series, evolved the design of the Hi-Lux Pickup from a construction worker's to a California surfer's and added a versatile, lifestyle oriented 4Runner to the range. On the crossover side, a versatile Four Runner came together with the top wagon Sprinter Carib. Suzuki upgraded the spartan LJ-Jimny into the stylish SJ Samurai—which became an instant hit with the European well-to-do girl. Far removed from the rugged utility of the Land Cruiser heritage, Mitsubishi's 1983 Pajero had been redesigned into a dynamic lifestyle vehicle, intended for outdoor fun and sports lovers, but also giving the feeling of a normal car that could be enjoyed during everyday commuting. Even more edgy in terms of style and comfort was the Nissan EXA, a compact multipurpose vehicle sporting—beyond the inevitable pop-up headlights—a modular roof section, which enabled a choice of coupé, pickup, convertible, or sports van. Within the history of Japanese car design, the flatster '80s can unquestionably be described as the heyday. The ultimate expression of this design ethos appeared in the form of race cars, justly called Super Silhouette: vertically lowered, horizontally stretched, with their technical protuberances expanded beyond what was deemed

Nissan Silvia Super Silhouette, 1983

Nissan Safari, 1980

Suzuki SJ 410, 1982

Toyota Soarer, 1981 / *bōsōzoku* 2010

Toyota Hi-Lux 4WD, 1983

Mitsubishi Pajero, 1983

acceptable, they are rare manifestations of *hade*, that very unusual aesthetic principle of the sympathetically loud—and to be appropriated by the *bōsōzoku* style later on. What the unknowing eye fails to acknowledge in the car design of the '80s, especially from Japan, is that the highest manufacturing quality was required to press and assemble the flattest and slimmest surfaces. The lesson of the modernist avant-garde perfectly suited the original *jimi* aesthetic principles of the Japanese: "Good taste in an understated, plain style." The beautifully balanced, both smooth and muscular Isuzu Piazza, penned by Giugiaro in 1979 as the Asso di Fiori concept car may have set a direction which all the Japanese followed during the '80s. When Nissan presented their CUE-X concept in 1985, it became clear that the lesson had been more than understood. Against the sleek, flat and slim hi-tech limousine from Japan Pininfarina's exceptional Ferrari Pinin now appears heavy if not clumsy. Invigorated by the the dynamic of Full Flat years, Japanese car design took new, often even contrasting directions. With the industry evolving into global concerns, operating international design and manufacturing facilities, the much sought-after evidence of on intrinsic design Japan-ness was finally found—and about to be lost soon. Impermanent as the cherry blossom, as anything Japanese must be.

Isuzu Piazza Irmscher, 1984

Nissan CUE-X, 1985

Nissan CUE-X, 1985

Nissan Leopard TR-X hardtop coupé, 1980

Nissan Leopard TR-X hardtop sedan, 1980

Mazda 323, 1977

Toyota 1300 Starlet SE, 1978

Mitsubishi Colt, 1979

Toyota 1300 Starlet S, 1978

Mazda 626, 1979

Mazda 626 Coupé, 1979

Mitsubishi Galant Sigma, 1976,

Mitsubishi Galant Coupé, 1979

Mitsubishi Sapporo, 1979

Mazda Luce, 1981

Toyota Camry, 1982

Mazda Cosmo, 1981

Toyota Celica LB Twin Cam 16, 1983

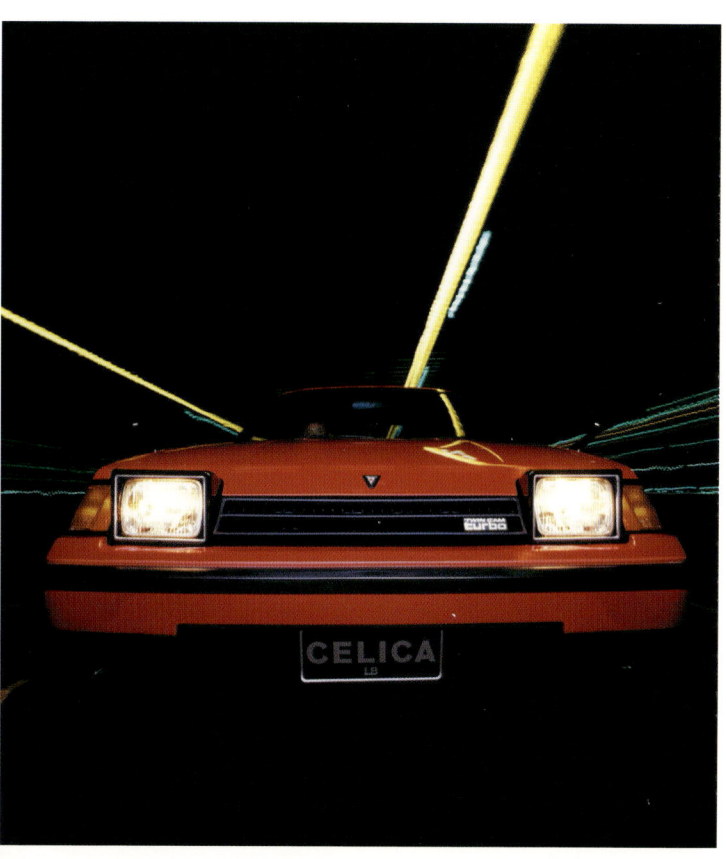

Toyota Celica LB Twin Cam Turbo, 1982
Toyota Celica XX Twin Cam 24, 1983

Toyota Soarer, 1981

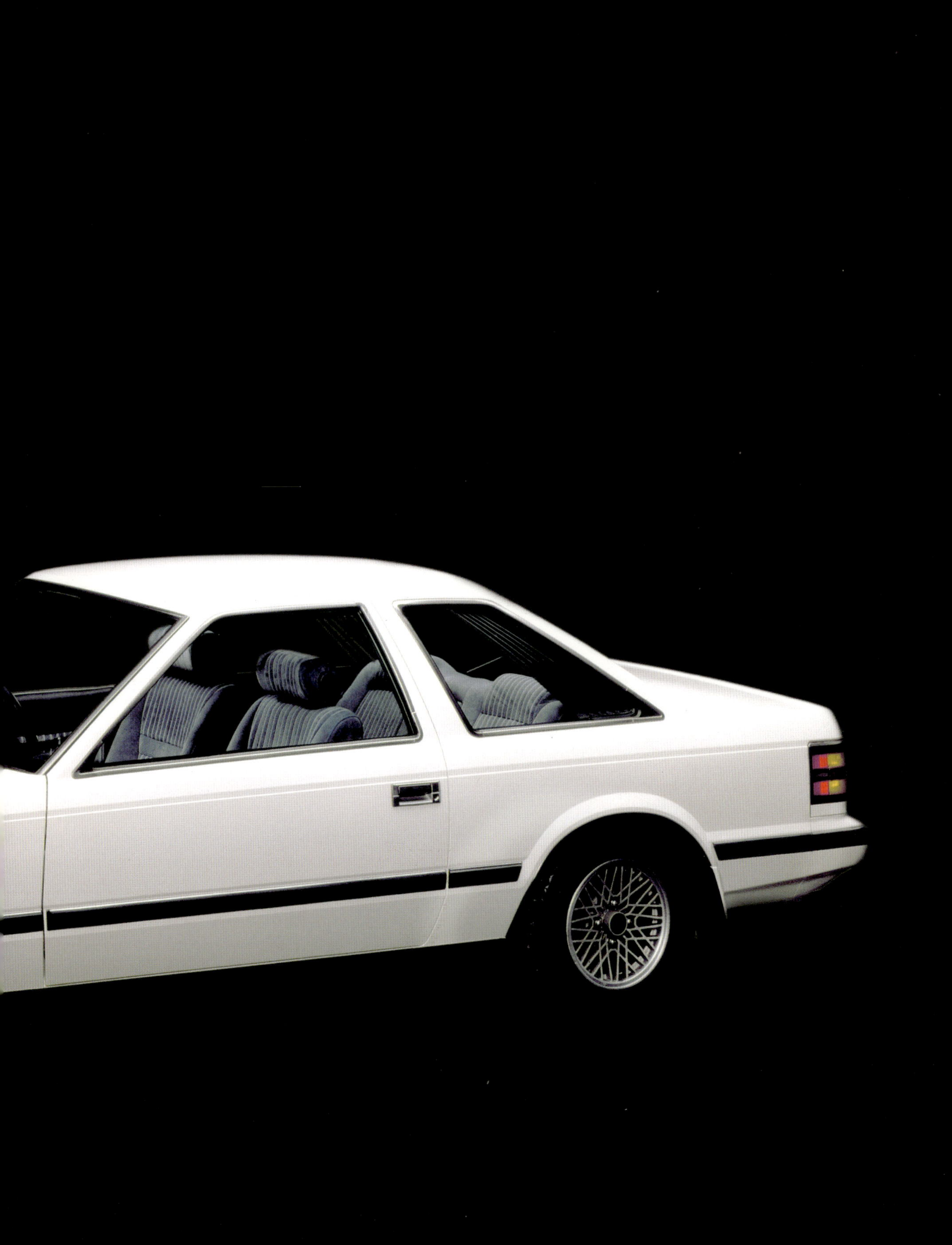

BOSOZOKU

Unlike their motorbike-riding next of kin—outcast gangs wreaking havoc on Japanese roads—the car-driving *bōsōzoku* can hardly be described as a "reckless tribe"—which is the literal translation of the term. The cars may be loud, visually as well as acoustically, but *bōsōzoku* aims not to intimidate or tease—the gatherings of this most Japanese car costume play community are more of an exhibition of good-natured outrageousness. The cars' make-up is crassly over the top and utterly useless in terms of performance. Doubtless, it is obviously impractical and hence mocking the automobile itself and its usual regalia of power and performance. The noise, the flared wings, the artfully

Nissan Skyline GTX-E 1972 / *bōsōzoku* 2010

silly exhausts, the snow shovel-sized front spoilers—much ado about not an awful lot.

Bōsōzoku is not about who is fastest or who is most powerful, but who goes the furthest in the pursuit of ridiculous extravagance. It is completely *hade*, like *pachinko* on wheel. Like any subculture worth its salt, *bōsōzoku* contains a number of subdivisions. Faintly related to motorsports are *kyūsha* and *yankii* styles—the former evoking exaggerated memories of 1970s Japanese sports cars; the latter inspired by the Japanese view of American fashion of the 1970s and '80s. Both these styles are based upon the basic *shakotan* look, which simply stands for low and wide—inspired by the Super Silhouette racers of the '80s. Thoroughbred *bōsōzoku* is a culmination of them all, escalating into a shrill parody of the sports car.

Nissan Pulsar EXA Turbo, 1983

Toyota MR2, 1984

Mazda 323 Sport Europe, 1983

Nissan March Super Turbo, 1989   Honda City Turbo II, 1983

Toyota Carina 1800 GT-TR, 1982

Nissan Pulsar Milano X1, 1984

VANS

In a country where living space is scarce and private housing beyond the reach of many, the van represents more than mere mobile utility. It is the projection of one's own aspirations for both intimacy and independency. Differentiation form the Western standard began with the size: just above the microscopic *kei tora*—the light truck out of which the Tall Boy would emerge—a full lineup was created. Toyota's range between the MiniAce and the full size HiAce would include the LiteAce, the TownAce and the more sophisticated MasterAce. Maintaining the cab-over layout throughout the '80s, these cars' designs evolved the typical white goods image of the delivery van, creating individual environments, either classy or sporty—and obviously incorporating 4x4 technology. Following the general trend, the semi-cab-over layout became fashionable by the mid-1990s, and with it a more urban, posh and glossy image. Today, the Japanese road is unimaginable without its multitude of fancy vans, a phenomenon which proved popular throughout all of Asia.

Toyota Master Ace, 1982

Honda Acty Street L, 1983

Subaru Domingo, 1984

Nissan Largo Umibouzu Limited Edition, 1985

Honda Accord Aerodeck, 1985

Honda Prelude, 1982

Honda Ballade Sports CR-X, 1983

HONDA

Ever the dreamer, Honda, after having experimented with nasty minicars, saw its peculiar approach towards car making paying off dividends in the 1980s. The first Civic and Accord models had been smash hits, in no small part thanks to the combination of the proven and tested front wheel drive layout and the unique CVCC engine technology, which enabled Honda to meet strict Californian emission standards without having to fit any catalytic converter. With its quality and engineering capabilities thereby proven, Honda set about conquering yet another sector: style. Employing—without officially declaring it—the services of legendary Italian design house, Pininfarina, for guidance, Honda developed the first cohesive corporate identity of any Japanese car brand. Its 1980s range sits at the forefront of the cool, technology-inspired styling *en vogue* at the time, both lending credence to and exhibiting the engineering underneath the sleek sheet metal. Honda's technological finesse is finally highlighted when the Japanese presented their own Ferrari—the NSX. Honda triumphs by marrying the mundane with the exceptional and redefines what a fast and capable, but also reliable and usable sports car should be like. The Italian and German competition is left awestruck.

Full Flat 166

Honda Civic Shuttle, 1983

Toyota Sprinter Carib, 1982

Nissan Prairie 4WD Nordica, 1987

Mitsubishi Space Wagon, 1983

Nissan Safari Turbo, 1985

Mitsubishi Pajero, 1983

Toyota Land Cruiser J6 & J7 lineup, 1987

LAND CRUISER

A versatile jeep endowed with the power of a truck, Toyota's original Land Cruiser is pretty much the off-road equivalent of the muscle car—before any muscle car. The lineup evolves into an impressive array of derivatives over the years, culminating in the square, iconic 1980s J7, catering to those who need the ultimate in cross-country ability and ruggedness. Finally, it gets immortalized as the 2006 FJ retro lifestyle Cruiser. Faithful to the old claim that it "gets you there, gets you back"—no matter if acting as unfailing survival tool to UN forces, as military truck or as poseurs' embodiment of the macho machine—the real Land Cruiser is regarded as a jack of all trades, all over the globe. Its lengthy bonnet badge has become synonymous with both the most utilitarian and the most preposterous appliance of the automobile—if the world car ever existed, then this must be it.

TOYOTA
TOYOTA
TOYOTA
TOYOTA
TOYOTA
LAND CRUISER
LAND CRUISER

Nissan Cefiro, 1988

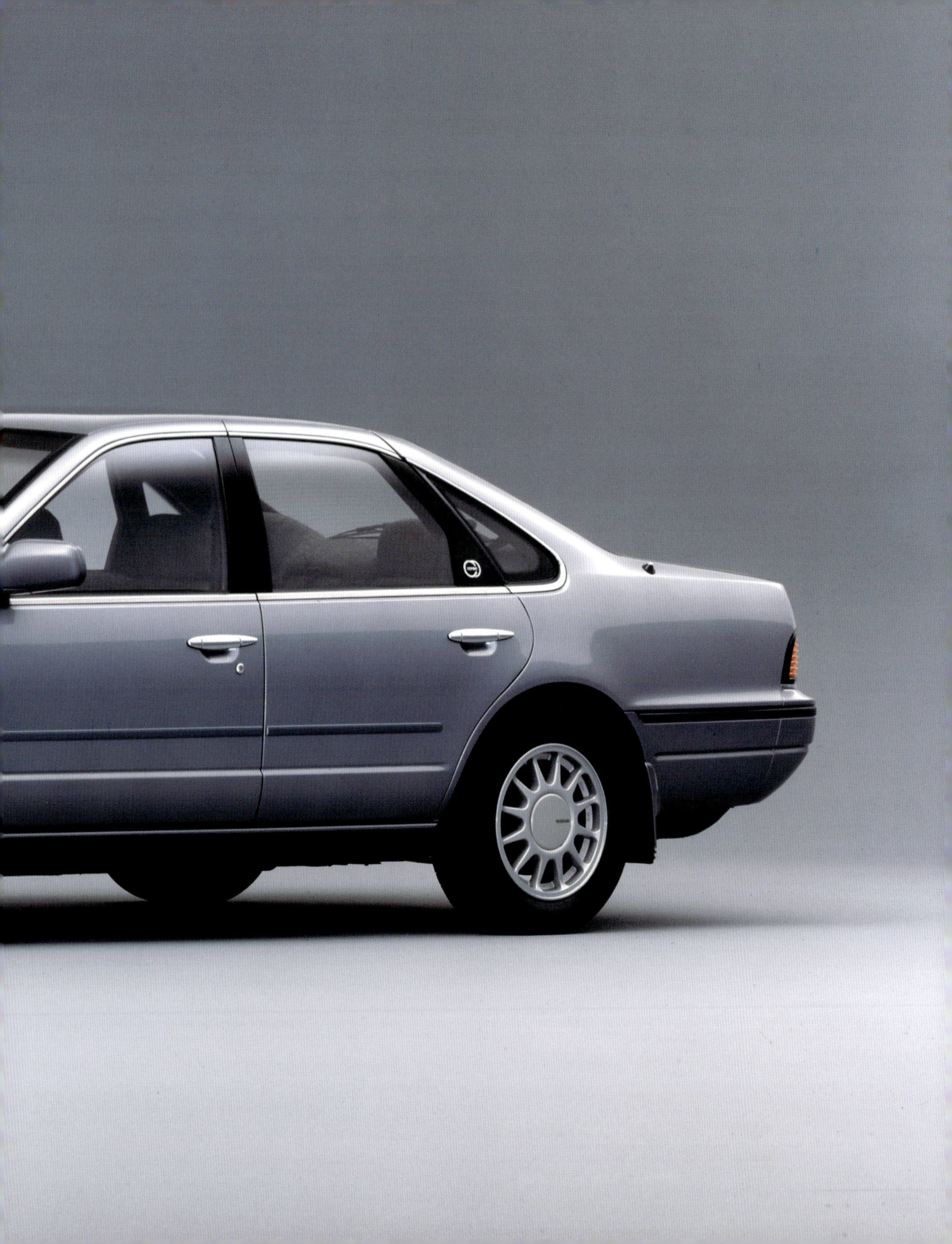

CELICA

ANIMOTION

The Japanese never kissed—at least not in public. Until the West came along, they knew a lot about sex, but nothing about love. Just as they would not understand an act of reciprocal and equal affection between men and the less equal women, kissing was actually forbidden by law until 1946. The Japanese sentimental education had but one great teacher: Walt Disney. Snow White and her Prince's example was assumed and reproduced without too deep an involvement, rather like some exotic form of acting. Japan also experienced no sexual and cultural revolution, unlike the West in the wake of the pill and the '68 movement. This was, first of all, due to sexuality never having been linked to sin. A second and most important factor may have been that in the 1960s, Japanese society was not ready yet. Thirdly, everybody was too busy making anything—including cars—but love. This meant the hidden conflict between men and women—or, better, the problem women had with the men's role—was never discussed in public, but instead individualized and transposed into the realm of fiction. Manga—particularly female manga writers since the '70s—and later on anime films were the driving forces of an unspoken revolution, aiming for a new societal setup. As Sharon Kinsella puts it: "The little girl heroines of rorikon manga—with large eyes and a body that is both voluptuous and child-like—reflect simultaneously an awareness of the increasing power and centrality of young women in society, and also a reactive desire to see these young women disarmed, infantilized, and subordinated." With attendance to the Comic Market growing from 600 in 1973 to 250,000 individuals in 1990, and Shogakukan publishers issuing twenty million copies of its magazines a month, the manga movement culminated in a profound social imbalance come the '90s.

Meanwhile, Japan's economy was speeding up after the Plaza Accord in 1985, boosting a gigantic, but short-lived Bubble Economy. Growing was also the salary of the *sararīmen*, who found themselves indulging in pleasures previously unheard of. Their business dress was now provided by the trendiest Italian fashion labels that all added a

Toyota Celica, 1993

men's line for the Japanese. On top of a very tight work schedule, playing golf came right ahead of offshore holidays, as the new social must. As an occasional refuge from the flood of nouvelle cuisine, the quality of sushi was visually enhanced by sprinkles of 24K gold leaves. An automobile of matching breed and visible status was demanded to perfect the *iki*—Japanese for cool—image of a new class of self-indulgent, if not simply selfish Japanese male individuals. In the TV spots of its day, the male car owner, in impossibly cool pose, is inevitably rewarded the silent company of a beautiful woman of European stature. The woman and the car serve the successful superiority of the male character—with the accompanying classical music or Ella Fitzgerald tunes emphasizing his taste. In "the age of the Legacy" or the "Grand Age" of the Gloria, the man could have it all. He just needed to choose whether he wanted it served inside his "private coupé" Leopard or within the "sedan freedom" of his Eterna. And if the "since 1968" mark on the Laurel appeared questionable, then there was simply no mistaking the plot behind the Honda Vigor's commercial: the car has Italian number plates, the French style mansion is huge, the telephone rings, and the golden Dupont lights up, as the call lady is just about to show up. She and Honda's potency-enhancing "FF Midship Straight 5" are "for men" only.

While cars in advertising had previously been seen discreetly cruising by or just moving slowly, the '80s suddenly substituted Ken and Mary for female idol, actor and racer Paul Newman, who declares: "The Skyline is terrific." Later on, a white RX-7 could be spotted dangerously speeding, even slightly drifting on wet country roads—a reminder of *The Graduate's* baby boomers' very unsocial attitude that goes beyond the road. Mazda's headline amounted to nothing short of sexual discrimination: "new adult sports"—the

Nissan Leopard, 1986

Honda Vigor, 1992

Subaru Legacy GT S2, 1991

Mazda Savanna RX-7 GT Limited, 1985

Nissan Skyline GT-ES "Paul Newman", 1983

word male being, of course, implicit. Unable to catch up, the OLs, the ever silent and silently discriminated office ladies, found refuge and finally emancipation in the realm of *kawaii*. As Sharon Kinsella explains, the trend had started during the '70s, with the development of a cryptic handwriting code—a mixture of English words, modified *katakana* logograms and symbolic icons—among youths. In a country that venerates calligraphy, the phenomenon was investigated and officially labeled as "Anomalous Female Teenage Handwriting." If one thing was anomalous, then it was the obvious fact that "these young people were rebelling against traditional Japanese culture and identifying with European culture, which they obviously imagined to be more fun." The fact of the matter is this: if the juniors had wanted to express love, they simply had no Japanese word for it. Using the heart as a symbol was the creative solution, from which the condensed, emoticonic global language originated that today enables smart digital communication. *Kawaii*'s style, Kinsella says, celebrated the "sweet, adorable, innocent, pure, simple, genuine, vulnerable." In a word: the cute. Gift card giant Sanrio went ahead and experimented with this new style, of which the ubiquitous *Hello Kitty* was to become the first and most successful interpretation. Like an avalanche of soft ice cream, pushed by TV and new magazines like *Cutie*, the market for *fanshi guzzu*—fancy goods—expanded to reach an estimated turnover of 10 billion dollars in 1990.

Sharon Kinsella perfectly describes the features of *kawaii* products: "Small, pastel, round, soft, loveable, not traditional Japanese, but a foreign style, dreamy, frilly, and fluffy." In *kawaii*, a growing public—and not just women, but increasingly young male adults, too—found an alternative, undeniably harmless form to express its individualism. Confronted with two options—

Hello Kitty, 1975

Olympus µ [mju:], 1991

Autozam Carol, 1989

Nissan Cima, 1988

cutting-edge class or soft mass—the Japanese brands made an inevitable choice: which was to serve both. As shall be seen further along, the conceptual gap turned out to be narrower than expected.

UPPER CARS

When it came to class, there was nothing new to be invented. Between 1985 and 1990, the import of premium and luxury brands skyrocketed: Audi, BMW, Ferrari, Lotus, and Mercedes-Benz tripled their sales; Cadillac, Jaguar, Maserati, Porsche, and Rolls-Royce grew by factor ten; Aston Martin, Bentley, and Lamborghini were new entries in a car market that grew by 65%, reaching 5,000,000 new registrations at the end of the decade. Luckily, the new premium liners that the Japanese were developing for their export markets would fit the plot perfectly. Flat design being too simple, too brutal and too Japanese, the need was felt to add a touch or two of aristocratic make-up to the affluent models that had been launched through the early eighties. First came Greek temple grilles, injections of chrome and branding paraphernalia, then a new generation of motor yachts-on-wheels. It was almost unilaterally agreed upon that the existing limitations in length and displacement—4.7 meters and 2 liters—which had dominated the design of all models, did not need to be obeyed anymore. Luxury had to be truly luxurious after all.

Towards the peak of the bubble, Nissan launched the ambitious Cima—peak in Italian, incidentally—of American hit fit appeal. Reserved for the US was the 1989 Infiniti Q45, a smooth motion symbol, incorporating Jaguaresque heritage. A stretched and more stately styled version of the Q45 would become the new President by Nissan Japan in 1990—with added eyes of a Jaguar XJ40.

Nissan Gloria, 1991

Although positioned two levels below, the flow line Gloria, new for 1991, was treated to a Bentley Eight's face and a Mercedes S-Class' bottom. Toyota was just as fast with its new flagship, called Toyota Celsior in Japan and exported as the Lexus LS400. Two years later, the Aristo followed. Both Toyota and Nissan had given rather straightforward names to their upper class brands: Lexus for *luxe* and Infiniti for infinite taste. But it was Honda who had been first to upgrade its lineup with Acura, standing for accurate—a range of badge-engineered Hondas with sporty, rather than luxury ambitions. New names were a necessity abroad, as all Japanese brands were considered too close to the low and middle class vehicles the American and European public had been accustomed to. The Lexus went about its mission by combining a potent stance with no-frills design that was remotely reminiscent of Mercedes-Benz only in its front end treatment. Although it was not of the strongest personality—which can be blamed on the Lexus' DNA having been neither Japanese nor European nor American—its design was a smooth, neutrally global effort, meant to reassure, rather than impress. And as if to confirm that this strategy was right, it turned out that indeed no one was impressed by the original Lexus style.

CUTE

Thrill and excitement appeared at the other end of the market, in the realm of cute. Here were the new proposals that would animate the flattened electrocardiogram of car enthusiasts worldwide. This stimulus' foreplay was reserved to the Japanese, who were presented with quite a revolutionary, flowing style in the guise of the charmingly smiling Honda Today of 1985. A limited edition Nissan Be-1 followed in 1987, the work of freelance

Acura Legend Coupé, 1987

Toyota Aristo, 1991

Lexus LS 400, 1989

industrial designer, Naoki Sakai. The Nissan looks and feels like a toy character, almost akin to its two-dimensional cartoon original even. It was offered in only four childish pastel colors and without any chrome. Thanks to its two big round eyes, one might think of retro, but due to the absence of a grille or mouth, one can "project one's feelings onto the character"—the *Hello Kitty* lesson being applied. And like *Hello Kitty*, this car was cute. The Nissan Pike series Be-1, Pao, S-Cargo—for *escargot*—and Figaro were one-of-a-kind experimental cars. Most important of them all were the rustic Pao and the bohemian Figaro—come 1991, way before others would even think of it, the retro trend had thus been established.

Even if the European considered it a provocation, original Japanese retro actually had nothing to do with the reanimation of the old—that came much later—but was an eminently new fashion of Western ambition, which matured into a long-lasting style. Limited though they were, Nissan's Pikes were '90s style, three-dimensional advertising and clever product placement at the same time. Those qualities also meant that there could have been no better marketing launch platform for Nissan's new March. The changes from the 1982 model were radical: gone was the angular flatness, making way for the cutest of all minis. What seems too plainly soft today felt like the most luring design kiss back in 1992. This was also the first Japanese car to get—among many other accolades—the European Car of the Year Award. Building on the *paikuka* personalization strategy, Nissan also offered the March as the retro-faced Autech Bolero. Outdoing them all in the eccentricity stakes was the improbable Jaguar Mark II into which Mitsuoka transformed the March.

The peak of cute was a little global car, designed in California and sold as Eunos Roadster in Japan, Mazda Miata in the US and MX-5 in Europe.

Autozam Revue, 1990

Honda Today, 1985

Nissan Be-1, 1987

When the first picture of it reached the media in 1989—depicting a red, smooth soap bar with fleshy lips and pop-up eyes—one simply could not believe that this dream car was actually true. The Miata built upon Honda's CR-X idea of the simple and economical sports car. But it was a roadster, the first after many years. And it was cute. Much has been speculated about the design of the world's most successful open sports car. From a Western perspective, it was a retro mix of Lotus Elan and Jaguar E-Type—even though the design team admitted to have been inspired by the humble Triumph Spitfire. From an Eastern perspective, it was simply new and cute—and, as chief designer, Shigenori Fukuda, explained to *Joyful Life* magazine in 1989: "A small, softly curved, comfortable car that would be a kind of friend, like a puppy." Following Aristotle's logic: if retro is soft and cute is soft, then cute is retro. Retro, as it was understood after the remake of the Range Rover, the Mustang and the Camaro, does not have to be soft though. Accordingly, soft was not solely cute. When they looked back at the classic style of the European heritage brands, Japanese designers saw softness. When they looked around at the *kawaii* phenomenon, they saw softness, too. Lastly, coming out of the '80s, with all their orthogonal flatness, and looking forward to the possibilities NURBS—Silicon Graphics' non-uniform, rational B-splines, the complex, computer-generated curved surfaces revealed in 1989—could afford, they could not help but see softness. While definitely stylish, Japanese soft lines remained intrinsically hi-tech, as demonstrated by the ergonomic and functional compactness of the Olympus μ [mju:] camera, a global design milestone.

In the same year as the Miata, the Toyota Celica had been improved into a completely rounded design. Its muscular build, black twin blade grille

Eunos Roadster, 1989

Triumph Spitfire 1500, 1974-80    Toyota Celica, 1989

and built-in spoiler deprived the sports car of its cuteness. Just as the Mark 2 Nissan March had changed from edge to cute, the California-designed Mark 2 Toyota Soarer—worldwide known as the Lexus SC 300—changed from edge to soft—despite its sheer size and fiery face prohibiting any impression of cuteness. Rather than cute, soft turned into the new reference: the MR2, the RX-7, the ZX, the Alcyone XT (now called SVX)—all these monuments of (w)edge flatness got soft curves in the '90s. Yet each one was different: the Toyota muscular, the Mazda flexuous, the Nissan tense, the Subaru spacy. The same freedom of identity also applies to the Xedos 6 or the Nissan Leopard J Ferie. Each of these cars may be retro, futuristic, or cute at the same time. And all of them were clearly soft. So the soft lines, soft surfaces, soft shapes pioneered by the Japanese became the ultimate '90s styling trend, and the last global design language, too. From the cute cars through the Porsche Boxster and Audi TT to the Alfa Romeo 156, Japanese animotion had proven itself to be capable of influencing outstanding automobiles. A minor side effect of this manifested itself in the shocking round headlamps which appeared on the Mercedes-Benz E-Class for 1995. But this global strength of the trend was at the same time its major weakness. After the cute avalanche of vanilla ice cream and design smarties had gushed out over the world's car bodies, the view was the same as that of an airport parking lot after a snowstorm: desolate rows of softly whitened creatures—all looking alike. To rescue the car, designers now had no other option than to start carving new identities through the sticky frost.

Nissan 300ZX, 1989

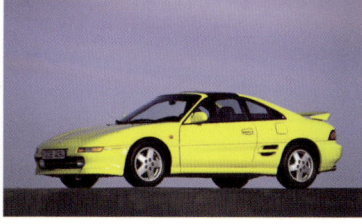

Toyota MR2, 1989

Mazda MX-6, 1992

Nissan Leopard J Ferie, 1992

Nissan Avenir Wagon, 1990

Lexus SC 300, 1991

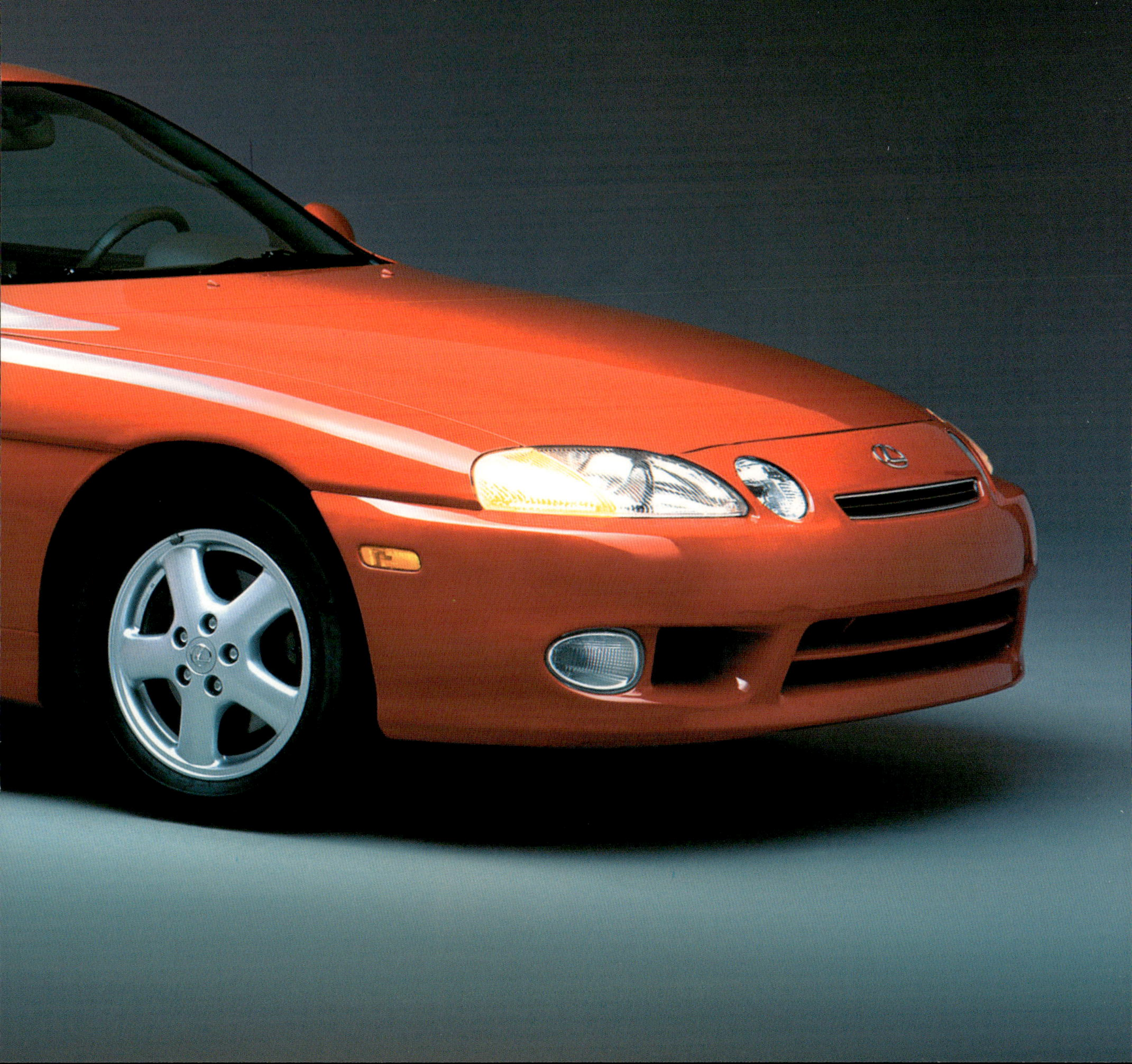

Nissan Cima, 1988

Nissan Cedric Brougham VIP, 1987

Mazda Luce Rotary Turbo hardtop, 1987

Toyota Corona Exiv, 1989

Infiniti Q45, 1989

Animotion 186

Nissan Cedric YPY, 1991

Toyota Crown Comfort, 1995

Toyota Crown Majesta, 1991

Acura Legend, 1995

ACURA

In 1986, having firmly established itself as a serious force to be reckoned with in the mass market, Honda aimed, if not for the stars, then at least for the upper echelons of the automotive stratosphere. As technology alone counted for little without prestige in this rarefied realm, a new name ought

accuracy. With two models, the Legend executive saloon (developed in cooperation with Rover of Britain) and smaller Integra, Honda set about entering the sporty side of the US prestige market. Both were welcomed with open arms, thus establishing a formula that would be used to even greater effect by

Acura Integra Type R, 2000
Acura Integra, 1996

Suzuki Cappuccino, 1991

ABC ROADSTER

When Mazda's Autozam AZ-1, Honda's Beat and Suzuki's Cappuccino arrived at the dawn of the 1990s, they were facing a rather daunting challenge. The yuppies they had been designed for had disappeared amid the bursting of the economic bubble. The times had changed so much that even these small fun cars' hedonism was suddenly deemed unacceptable. These three roadsters may have looked endearingly innocent, but that could not distract from their guilt-laden nature, for they were the progeny of a sinful era that could only be overcome through austerity. With their hi-tech paraphernalia of gullwing doors, turbochargers, mid-engines or t-tops, these adorable creations constituted the most unique manifestations of the Japanese automobile.

Autozam AZ-1, 1992

Honda Beat, 1991

Autozam Carol, 1989

CUTE CAR

Opposites attract. That is the simplest explanation for how *kawaii*, once a mere whimsical trend, could turn into one of the pillars of Japanese pop culture. Not only pre-adolescents find themselves falling for *kawaii's* charms, and not even just females: the Cute car's looks have been feminized, if not infantilized, like there is no tomorrow. It became more anthropomorphic than ever before, its attributes being cute and adorable, rather than the luscious and lascivious

Subaru Vivio T-top, 1993

Nissan March, 1992

of yore. The femme fatale à la Fairlady Z has been sent home, for a little girl in school uniform—the Miata—to take her place as the object of affection. Hence cute cars do not seduce, but endear themselves in naive ways—one trait among others shared with retro cars. Which is why Nissan's 2002 March, usually candy-colored, looks at the road through goggle-eyes more likely to make the owner want to caress it tenderly than throw it into a curve.

Suzuki Twin, 2003

Nissan Be-1, 1987
Autech Nissan March Tango, 1997

Nissan Figaro, 1991
Nissan S-Cargo, 1989

Nissan Pao, 1989

Autech Nissan March Bolero, 1999

PAIKUKA

Limited in size and availability, *paikuka*—derived from the English term "pike car"—is defined by a whimsical historicism that is undeniably cute and overwhelmingly nostalgic. Using classical, mostly European design cues and applying them onto distinctly Japanese *kei* cars makes for a peculiar look that is best interpreted as a self-deprecating homage.

But *paikuka* aesthetics are not one-sided—they range from miniaturized duplicates—such as Mitsuoka's British-inspired models—to post-modern stylistic references. The latter category—including Nissan's Figaro or the WiLL Vi—is nothing other than a precursor of the global new romanticism.

EUNOS

Causing the biggest stir among Mazda's collection of new brands for the '90s is the "fun to drive" Eunos, thanks to some outstanding products, most notably the Eunos Cosmo coupé and the Eunos Roadster—Miata or MX-5 on foreign shores. Both these cars showcase the maturity and sophistication the Japanese automobile has reached. The difference between them is that the Cosmo, a technological marvel clad in elegant, understated sheet metal, remains a connoisseur's choice, while the Roadster immediately turns into a phenomenon, an instant classic. That is not just due to its harking back to the traditional British roadster recipe or its paying homage to some of the familiar styling cues of open top motoring: this is a cute car by all means. The Roadster evokes not just the looks, but the actual feeling of a time when cars were allowed to be unashamed fun and a man's—or woman's—best friend. After reconsidering the need for quite so many brands, Eunos was discontinued in 1996.

Eunos Cosmo, 1990

Eunos Roadster S Limited, 1993

Eunos Roadster V Special, 1990

EFINI

At the dawn of the 1990s, when Mazda's intricate rebranding exercise was in full swing, it was decided that, above the entry level Autozam and the sporty Eunos, a luxury oriented counterpart with a dashing image was needed. The resulting Efini badge was a curiously ethereal solution. The name's pronunciation, based on the French *infini*, or infinity, hinted at an almost spiritual connotation that seemed at odds with the cars themselves, which were based on existing, down-to-earth Mazda models. Indeed, this kind of romanticism appears to have been lost, since Efini as a car brand soon entered the realm of forgotten badges and today only serves as a name for a Mazda dealership chain.

Efini RX-7, 1991

Mazda Xedos 6, 1991

MAZDA

As a David amongst the Goliaths Nissan and Toyota, Mazda needed to be particularly resourceful and creative. This tactic also meant that the company had to take risks—a trait that saw Mazda embrace idiosyncratic technologies, such as Felix Wankel's rotary engine, the big boys would shy away from. Selling by the hundreds of thousands before the oil crisis, the RX range of rotary-engined sports cars still enjoyed long-lasting success in its aftermath, including a triumph at Le Mans in 1991, which demonstrated how such foolhardy perseverance can pay off. Equally querulent, and at least as rewarding, was Mazda's decision to revive a breed of car that was, at the end of the 1980s, as dead as the dodo: the roadster. The overwhelming success of the Miata/MX-5/Roadster may remain Mazda's greatest achievement, but it also heralded a fertile era, as showcased by models ranging from the exotic 323 Astina to the beautiful Eunos Cosmo. As far as design research is concerned, Mazda forcefully embodies the brand's "zoom-zoom" anthem. The move towards soft lines in the '90s—as exhibited by the Capella, RX-7 and Autozam Revue models—reset standards within the industry. Later on, the flowing Nagare waves washed ashore, courtesy of Laurens van den Acker—as seen on the Mazda 5—soon to be followed by Ikuo Maeda's KODO, the "Soul of Motion", on sale today.

Animotion   200

Mazda Familia NEO, 1994

Mazda Roadster "10th Anniversary Model", 1998

Mazda Lantis, 1993

Mazda Millenia "25M", 2000

Suzuki Jimny Cabrio, 1998

Suzuki Jimny, 1998

SUZUKI

As if to conform to its motorbike heritage, Suzuki hardly ever went beyond being considered a *kei* car specialist—for this family business never built any automobile larger than a mid-size sedan. Possibly the result of a long-lasting relationship with Giorgetto Giugiaro, the tall 1993 Wagon R quickly became a bestseller. But Suzuki's global image was actually shaped by fun and games—or rather by the SJ mini jeep, which introduced the masses to the fun side of 4x4 vehicles. What was born as a Japanese commercial vehicle hence became an international lifestyle car. Almost a decade later, in 1989, Suzuki began offering a domesticated variant of the same breed, the Escudo. This car spelled out the recipe that would spread across the entire automotive landscape over the coming years: take the utility vehicle's sense of adventure, nurture its non-conformist flair and make concessions to everyday necessities. Here you have the SUV.

Suzuki Escudo, 1988

Suzuki X-90, 1996

Subaru Alcyone SVX, 1991

SUBARU

One of the "six diamonds" of the heavyweight Fuji Heavy Industries, Subaru distinguishes itself by being both idiosyncratic and contradictory. The brand DNA is there and present, thanks to Subaru's status as a pioneer of all-wheel drive, a full decade before the term Quattro meant anything other than just four in Italian. The company's unremitting devotion to boxer engines being another case in point, Subaru can rightfully claim to be genuinely different from the Japanese automotive herd. Yet the distinctiveness of its engineering stands in marked contrast to Subaru's styling. Mostly anonymous, with the odd burst of eccentricity—think the Alcyone—Subaru's design language has been utterly contrary to the values of its engineering. It is as though this anti-fashion attitude was actually perfectly appreciated by its clientele—evoking Saab's standing—since Subaru owners remain among the most loyal and satisfied of any car brand. And as though size—or style—really did not matter, the plain Impreza even made it into one of the most exotic, because undeniably unobtrusive, of all sports cars.

Subaru Impreza Sports Wagon, 1992

Daewoo Nubira Station Wagon, 1997

DAEWOO

Long since forgotten, Daewoo, automotive branch of a *chaebol* of the same name, had actually been at the forefront of the South Korean car stampede of the 1990s. In some ways, the company was a pioneer, not least regarding styling. Starting with the 1996 Lanos, Daewoo could boast the first consistent corporate identity of any South Korean car brand, courtesy of designer, Giorgetto Giugiaro. He went on to style a few more Daewoos, most significantly the cheeky Matiz in 1998, which had started its life as a city car proposal that had been rejected by Fiat. Other Italians also dabbled in the Daewoos range, Pininfarina or I.DE.A among them, with a German—head of engineering, Ulrich Bez—keeping a watchful eye on proceedings. Alas, this progressive, globalized approach came to naught when the mighty Daewoo *chaebol* went under, leaving Daewoo Motors struggling until GM stepped in.

Daewoo Lanos, 2000

Daewoo Matiz, 1998

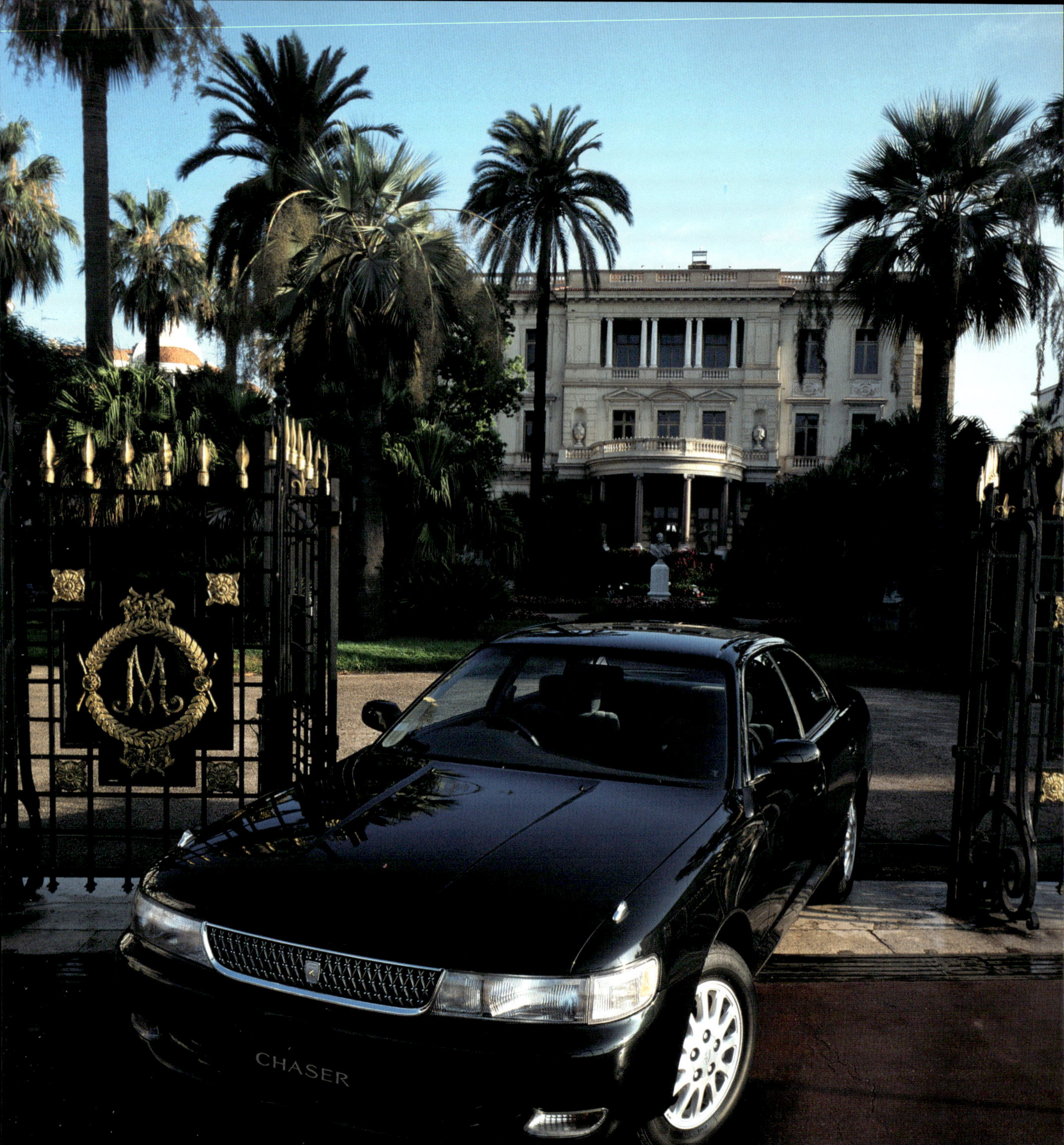
CHASER

Toyota Curren, 1995

Toyota RAV4 L, 1998

Toyota Sprinter Marino, 1992

Mazda 626, 1992

Toyota Estima Super Charger, 1996

Nissan Serena, 1991

Animotion   210

Toyota Supra, 1993

Hyundai Coupé, 1999

Toyota Sera, 1990

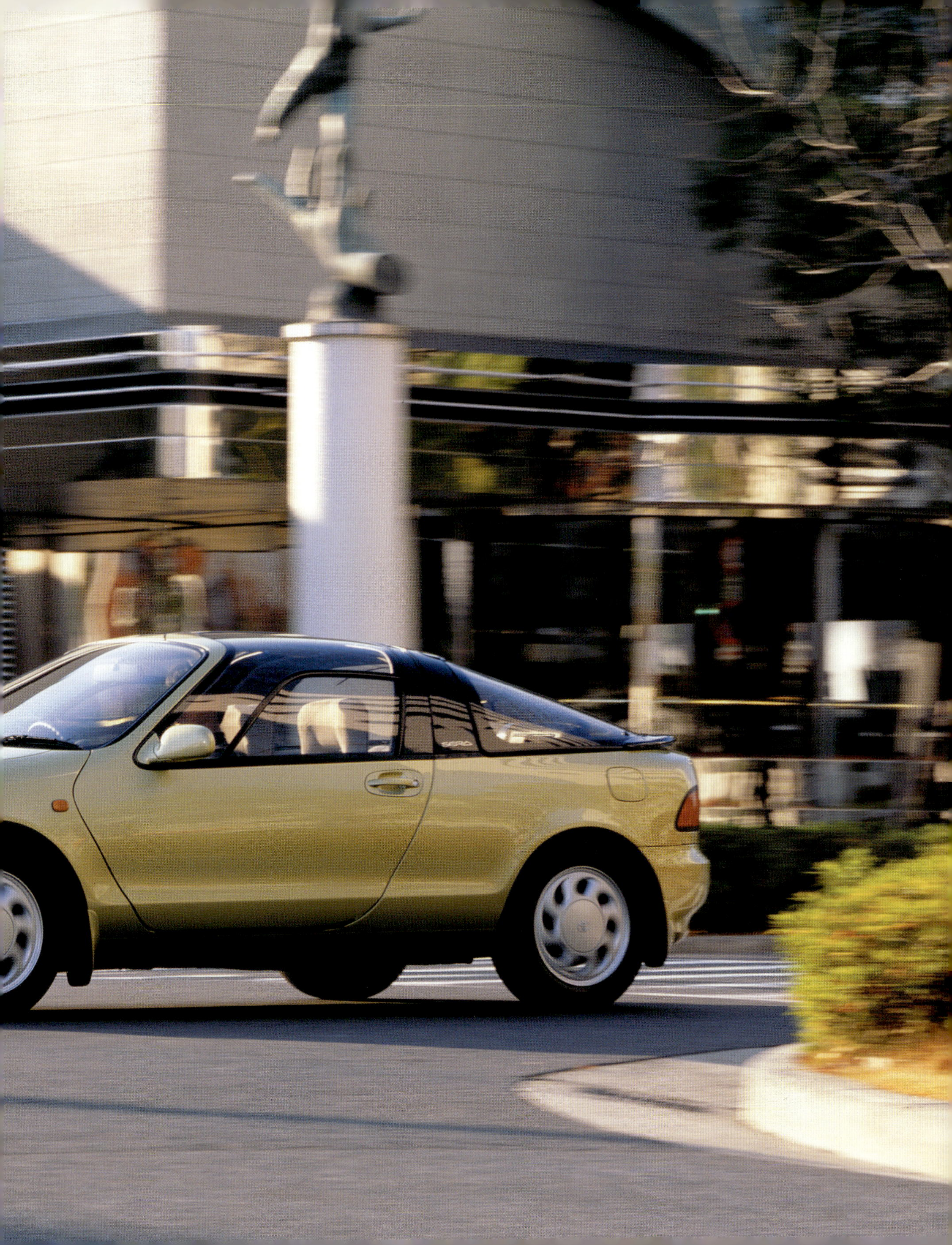

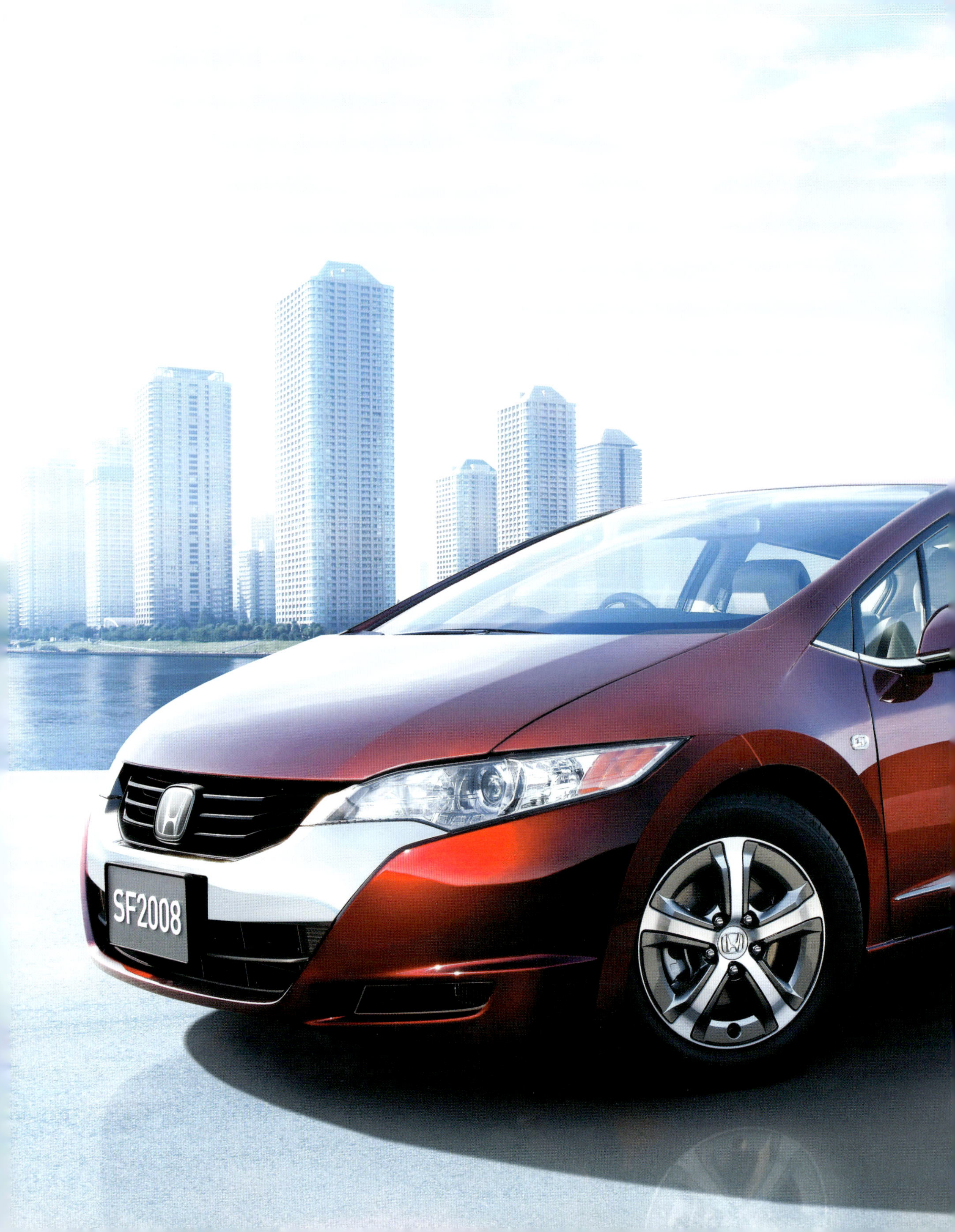
SF2008

HY BREED

When the bubble economy burst in 1990, the Japanese fell into social despair, calling the following ten years a Lost Decade, only to find themselves having to extend the term to The Lost Twenty Years. If one image were capable of portraying the global economy's roller-coaster ride, then it would have to be the chart of the Nikkei 225 index. Having steadily increased towards the 13,000 mark by the end of 1985, the Nikkei finally reached an all-time high of 39,000 points four years later. In 1990, it dropped by 40%, to 24,000. Then it started looping and twisting and turning, diving downwards and lifting upwards through hammerheads, horseshoes, and batwings, dropping as low as 7,500 points in April 2003—that is 80% below the level of 1989—only to regain 40% within six months. The fact of the matter is that, starting in 1989, the world was becoming a different place. Gorbachev's perestroika led to the German Reunification in 1990 and the dissolution of the Soviet Union in 1991. In a climate of social uprising, Deng Xiaoping's economic reforms forced the reopening of the Shanghai Stock Exchange at the end of 1990, boosting the privatization of the economy, which would make her GDP skyrocket and turn China into the largest and most appealing of all the world's markets.

In comparatively small South Korea, where, in 1980, the gross domestic product per capita was a mere one-third of the Japanese, the government and industry agreed to invest in new technologies—above all in electronics. In 1988, after having won by 2:1 against Nagoya, Seoul hosted the second Summer Olympics to be held in Asia since the 1964 games in Tokyo. As though this had been an omen, uprising Samsung went about overtaking a weakening Sony—which even had to accept a British-born American CEO in 2005. Yet this could not prevent Samsung's market capitalization from becoming ten times higher than Sony's by the end of the Lost Two Decades. Accordingly, Forbes now ranks the South Korean brand as the 9th best of the world, while Sony has to take seat number 80. In a sense, Samsung was simply busy making better flat TV screens, smartphones, and

Honda FCX Clarity, 2008

refrigerators, while Sony was losing its touch with the mass market. Its Aibo robots, for example, were as technologically exceptional as they were of limited marketing value. As technology was dematerializing, so was the physical evidence of Japan's former success. Equally immaterial was the nostalgic spirit—partially shared with Western society—out of which many a retro-styled product would pop up across the '90s. The appropriation of past styles began as a kind of ingenious exploration within a new fashion, as demonstrated by the decorative Olympus Écru camera of 1991. Twenty years later, photographers on a shopping spree would find themselves taken back to a digitized version of the 1960s, thanks to stores being filled with remakes of classics like the Olympus Pen camera.

Japan had not lost this war, and neither had she lost a game—she had stopped being the Asian wunderkind. Perhaps even due to exhaustion after decades of work and a seemingly endless growth of her economy, the ageing country now had to compete, inside and outside the islands' borders, with financial ups and downs of a kind one single country could hardly ever control—as seen during the Asian financial crisis of 1997 and the global crisis ten years later. In fact, the messages from Japanese industry were, as a whole, not as bad, but simply contradictory—which may be even worse for the orderly Japanese. Between 1990 and 2010, the numbers of humble *kei* cars in use climbed from two to 17.5 million, making them the largest car category by far. Sales of luxury cars over 2 liters climbed too, from two to 11.5 million. But the three middle classes in-between were stalling, at just below 29 million. At the same time, new registrations had fallen from 5 to 4.2 million per year. A look into this mirror revealed that Japanese society was losing its middle class, the core of the country's economic

Sony Aibo, 1999

miracle, while gaining a new youth and an old upper class. Now that companies would lay off employees or even had to face insolvency, the myth of the workaholic *sararīman* suffered, the suicide rate rose, while the number of *freeter*—young people with no full-time job—increased rapidly. The consequences of all this cannot be interpreted univocally: On the one side, the fading out of traditional values and roles was lamented, bringing a typically Japanese attitude of self-denial to an end. But on the other side, a younger society, standing for personal freedom and daring creativity, could be welcomed as the beginnings of a de-Japanized, cosmopolitan attitude.

The arrival of the mobile phone played a crucial role in this spreading of a new way of living and consuming. Japan was among the first to adopt the new accessory, which quickly substituted manga and cigarettes as the preeminent pastime. Not surprisingly, Japan also had a new, hi-end technological solution for this tool ready before any other country. As early as 1999, NTT docomo's i-mode enabled mobile internet access, content sharing, live chats, and payment solutions. Long before Facebook reached the West, the *keitai denwa* transformed a shy, not really talkative people into networked social beings. The influence of this development was soon to be seen in youth fashion, where Just in time became the norm. Swarms of teens were now browsing the hundreds of upcoming styles presented every year at the boutiques of Tokyo's Shibuya and Ikebukuro districts, selecting what they considered the hippest and spreading the news over their phones. Trends were thus born and killed overnight. Donald Richie reports the words of the editors of *Popteen*, a fashion magazine that sold 500,000 copies a month: "By the time the magazine comes out, the fashion has already changed. Things move so fast, the only strategy is to keep changing." What is

Olympus Écru, 1991

more important is that these trends were rarely designed within marketing departments or by the occasional artistry of an Issey Miyake, but rather they originated from the very core of the market—they were therefore of a social and public nature. Among the hottest trends of the 2002 spring season were "bohemian, ethnic, Tyrolean knit, cyber trance, used touch, resort, relax, and cute conservative." Far removed from the rigidity of the kimono, the top hat, and the Armani suit, the new Japanese look was a mutant, global hybrid. As a further expression of the now spreading *kosupure*—Sunday's costume play—one would spot deeply tanned, tribal-looking *ganguro*, walking side by side with smart, blonde Barbie dolls. *Kawaii*, the plain cute, seemed to be but one stationary thing of the past. The new millennium's word for individual coolness is *yabai*—anything but univocal, it can mean different things at the same time, and is certainly not meant to indicate one precise style. It is much rather a combination of a certain individual with a certain look that may be called *yabai* at a certain moment by another individual. If one word can describe the evolution of Japanese car design across the hybrid 2000s, then *yabai* it is.

RETRONEWS

The Lost Twenty Years were equally contradictory to the world's largest automotive industry. Between 1990 and 2010, Suzuki and Daihatsu doubled their sales in Japan, Honda improved theirs by 20%, and Toyota lost 25%, while Mazda, Mitsubishi, and Nissan each lost 50%. Mazda handed control over to Ford in 1996, while Mitsubishi tried its luck signing an "alliance" agreement with DaimlerChrysler. But it was Nissan who was hit the hardest of them all. Not only had it lost the BC war against Toyota—at that time,

Toyopet Crown, 1955

Toyota Origin, 2000

selling three times as much in Japan—but now it also had to give up control over the company to Renault of France, who sent out French-Lebanese-Brazilian executive, Carlos Ghosn, as new CEO of Nissan in 2001.

Toyota, having surpassed GM as the world's largest manufacturer for 2007, found itself declaring losses the following year—for the first time in 71 years of business. The role model for permanence and conservativeness was also sending out a hybrid design message. Having always been looking forward to growth, this break then actually afforded Toyota a rare opportunity to look back, only to realize that there were ten generations of the Corolla—the world's bestselling car—and eleven generations of Crown sedans around. This in addition to 40 years of the Land Cruiser range and 33 years of the unique President—the most long-living and most classical of all state limousines. So the giant, who was selling 70 different models in Japan alone, suddenly found itself with a considerable heritage that required managing. A problem not uncommon to Nissan too, what with eleven generations of the Skyline, or Honda, with its seven generations of the Civic, or even Mitsubishi, thanks to also seven generations of the Lancer.

The first step of the hybrid mutant design strategy was the reanimation of the old. What had been born as just another form of costume play—the camouflage of *kei* cars to cater to the desire for Western style—evolved into the rediscovery and proposition of bygone Japanese automotive myths. Latently underlying this was the attempt to strengthen the Japanese brands against global attacks—either that, or it may have been a sign of nostalgic uncertainty that perfectly matched the spleen of those days. Speaking of style, going retro turned out to be a very powerful fuel injection into all Japanese brands. If the cute Miata

Toyota FJ Cruiser, 2003

Toyota Land Cruiser J4, 1980

had inspired the classicism of the Honda S2000 and the Suzuki Cappuccino, the Origin of 2000—a remake of the original Toyopet Crown—actually was Japan's first attempt at reproducing her own past, albeit taking the form of purely stylistic amusement. With its typically cartoony style, the 2003 remake of the original Land Cruiser earned itself a place as a kind of post-modern icon. In 2005, the third generation MX-5 surprised by replicating the styling features of the 1989 original in a unique kind of retro-retro. Ten years later, Honda would attempt the same by injecting the design DNA of the original N360 into the sexy N-ONE. Unique to this second stage of Japanese retro, as compared to the American and European takes on the theme, is the combination of vintage looks and contemporary, or even advanced design solutions: the rear opening doors on the FJ-Cruiser, the retractable hardtop of the MX-5, or the Tall Boy body of the N-ONE have nothing in common with the superficial styling of a new Beetle or Mini.

SUPERLINES

As if to prove that design was about to advance, stylistic research, led by the wish to sharpen the profile of all brands, was undertaken. Finally emerging at the end of the vanilla ice cream tunnel in 1999 were the sculpted lines and sharp detailing of the Toyota Altezza—or Lexus IS, standing for Individual and Sport. The Japanese added three-dimensional modeling to Ford's contemporary New Edge Design, without indulging in the latter's exaggerated graphics. Instead, the midsize sedan promoted clear glass tail lights, which were at once a new trend and a reminiscence of the 2000 GT. The new IS compelled the global competition—with BMW at the forefront—to redefine the benchmarks for standard sedan

Mazda Roadster, 2006

Honda S2000, 2006

Toyota Altezza, 1999

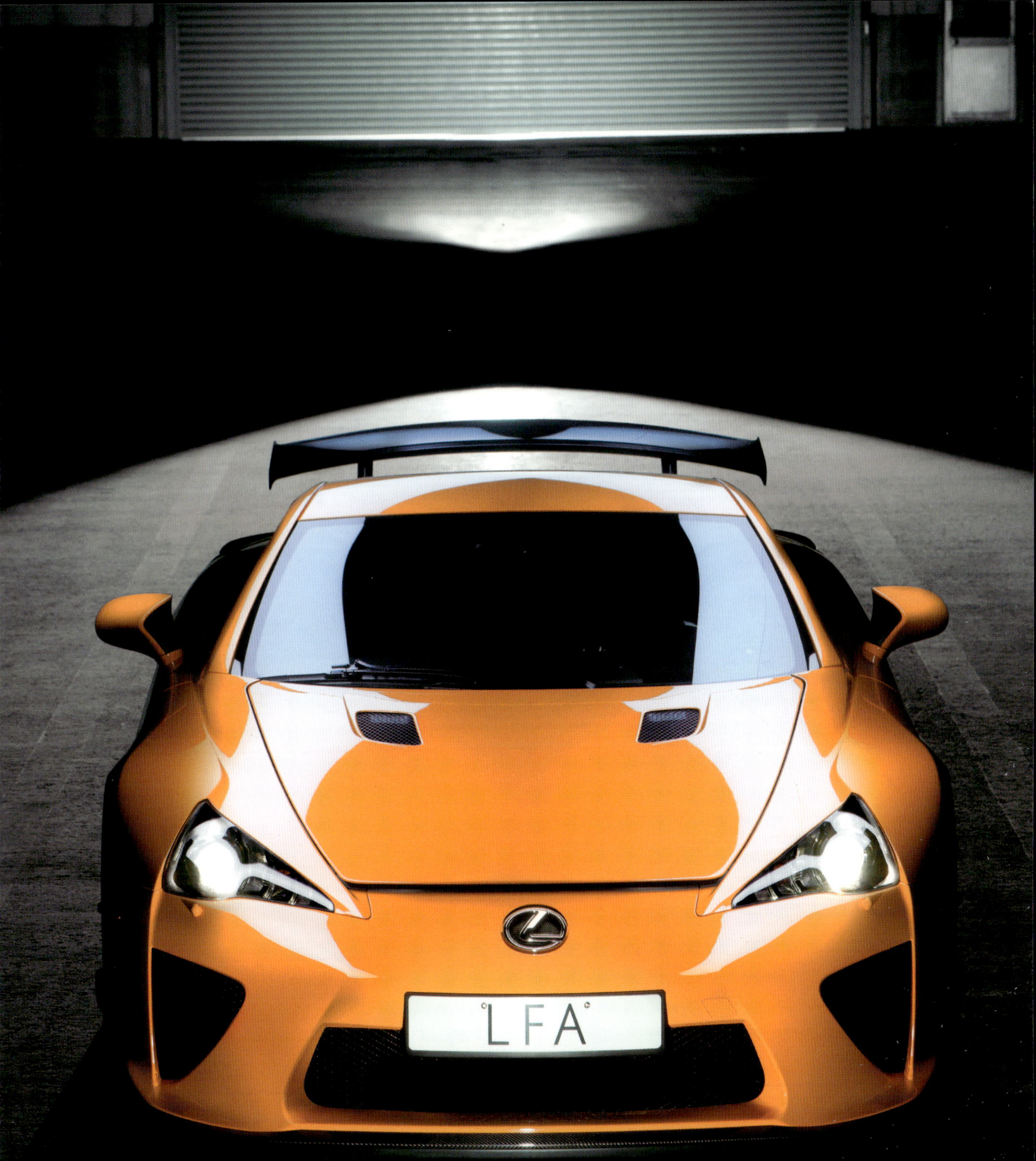
LFA

design. From that point on, Lexus design gradually evolved into L-Finesse, a first attempt at declaring the emancipation of a Japanese brand from Western design. The marketing department explained it as being a genuine combination of "intriguing elegance, incisive simplicity, and seamless anticipation." As for Toyota, the effort of defining a univocal design language was not even attempted on the domestic market: too wide was the product portfolio, too varied were the market niches. What the 1990s had revealed—besides the weaknesses of soft creations—was a collection of experiments, such as the advanced 1990 Sera, the sneaky 1994 RAV4, the nostalgic 1997 Corolla, the sharp 1999 Celica, or the smooth MR-2 of the same year. Now the new millennium afforded the customer the opportunity to appreciate the slightly animistic, reassuringly organic bodies of the European Toyotas—the Yaris, the Auris, the Avensis. The same slight traces of Shintō religion, albeit this time in more abstractly natural fashion, would also be found in Mazda's Nagare waves—courtesy of Dutch chief designer, Laurens van den Acker. A hidden spiritual link also seemed to connect the anthropomorphic lines of the 2003 Nissan March with the biomorphous shape of the 2010 HondaJet, which had been skillfully engineered to vaguely resemble a flying dolphin. Under the design leadership of Shiro Nakamura, Nissan quickly regained design ground by implementing a consistently sophisticated and thoroughly individual carved body line with strong graphical elements for its 2002 lineup, which included the Avenir, Murano, and new Fairlady Z. Given this much branding to cope with, no one could be surprised to find a great many diametrically opposed strategies. Toyota's WiLL was as precisely targeted at the individual, anti-automobile taste as the Muji Car 1000—a de-branded, spartan version of the Nissan March, sold

Toyota Corolla lineup, 1997

Nissan Murano, 2002

Honda HA-420 Hondajet, 2003

Toyota MR-2, 1999

Toyota Celica, 1999

Mazda 5, 2010

online by the trendy "no-brand" retail chain—seemed to be concerned with conveying an image of invisibility and disinterest. Nissan's Autech editions of equally de-branded, but aesthetically pimped-up series models finally seemed to try and reach for both extremes: individuality and anonymity.

By the same degree as the self-formatting global society seemed to find no style to agree upon, everything could and would now be *yabai* in Japan: the anonymous, the bold, the androgynous. As if to prove that "nothing is impossible," armies of designers were relying on extremely efficient production lines and strategically deployed sales channels to promote their work: no less than four—Toyota, Toyopet, Corolla, and Netz—in the case of Toyota, and three—Primo, Clio, and Verno—for Honda.

Mazda even went as far as proposing three different variations of its cute roadster, each with individual identity and visual detailing, all carrying the very same denomination of Roadster Coupé: Type S for Standard, Type E—note the wordplay—for elegant design and Type A for authentic race car design. Out of one simple midsize sedan, Toyota was able to conjure several identities. The Mark X, heir to the Corona Mk II, remained equally Jaguaresque in name, while stylistically turning into a Maserati-inspired direction. The Crown—unchanged in its design since 1979—was split into three individually styled types: the ambitious Royal, the more ambitious and sporty Athlete, and the even more ambitious and expensive Majesta. This quest for a new identity was as tormenting a process for car designers as it was to the rest of society. Crossbreeding of different personalities and body styles then gave birth to new crossover types: the versatile Fun Cargo and the practical Probox by Toyota, the loft-like Cube 3, experimental Rasheen, sporty

Mazda Roadster Coupé Type A, 2003

Mazda Roadster Coupé Type S, 2003

Nissan March, 2002

Toyota Mark X, 2006

Toyota Auris, 2006

Toyota Vitz, 2005

Dualis and androgynous Juke by Nissan, as well as the smart HR-V and the rugged Crossroad by Honda. Just as among the teenagers of Tokyo, all these proposals, although inhabiting the same sector, never shared a corresponding stylistic common thread. But then again, even in the case of as representative an object as the train, searching for the strict corporate identity of the Deutsche Bahn ICE speed trains—which are painted in the same style and same color, featuring the same red strip across all three generations of trains—would be impossible with Japan Railways. Excluding the original Bullet Train, one can spot six different styles—partially dictated by function—six different colors and six different stripes on Japan's high speed trains today. In the very same fashion, Toyota's brand strategy for Japan gradually evolved towards a very peculiar solution, in order to enhance individuality. With few exceptions, the global elliptical logo appears only on the back of the car: the grille, in contrast, is adorned with model-specific badges, each with a very different status and style. Besides the crown for the Crown models, one finds an X for the Mark X, a Nespresso-like N for the Noah, or a much more abstract, flowing N for models, such as the Wish, Voxy, or RAV4, that are sold through the premium Netz retail channel. Even more mysterious is the rapacious bird branding of Toyota's Harrier Hybrid SUV.

HYBRID

Amidst the many experiments, Japanese car design was finally about to converge with the invention—or, to be more precise: reinvention—of the hybrid shape. The idea of parallel hybrid technology can be traced back to the famed Californian Zero Emission Vehicle Act of 1990, which the Japanese took as seriously as only they could.

Toyota Fun Cargo, 2002

Honda Crossroad, 2007

Nissan Juke, 2010

Nissan Rasheen, 1994

Honda HR-V, 1999

Toyota Probox, 2002

Although DaimlerChrysler and General Motors were able to freeze the regulation, the Japanese kept to their plans to produce advanced technology, green hybrid vehicles—a concept all competitors actually rejected until it was almost too late for them. That was a few years after the Toyota Prius, a conventional compact sedan, had been launched in Japan in 1997. The Honda Insight, a sporty aerodynamic fastback coupé, was actually first to arrive in California in 1999—just before export of the Prius began. If the one was too conventional, the other was perhaps too special. Trying to come up with a solution to this problem, Toyota had the intuition to combine the sedan's packaging with the streamlined, unobtrusively futuristic line of the Honda. The resultant 2003 Prius may not have been the green car of the future, but it definitely looked like it was. In that very same year, movie stars like Harrison Ford adopted the strange Toyota to parade at the Academy Awards ceremony—and California immediately acclaimed the highly recognizable car as the new set of Hot Wheels.

Almost as an act of paying tribute, Honda soon reverted its own line of green vehicles—the Insight, the FCX Clarity, the CR-Z—to the original iconic silhouette. Critics may argue that the advanced aerodynamics is more of a stylistic than substantial nature, or that the sloping one-box limits both ease of access and functionality. But the obvious truth is that its emotional and symbolic value strongly contributes to the global acceptance of the hybrid shape—thereby certainly rendering it the most originally Japanese car typology. The best-selling car in Japan since 2009, with more than six million units sold worldwide, the Prius can rightfully claim to have established itself as the first and latest global design icon. Demonstrating the uniqueness of the phenomenon is another contemporary iconic shape: the Tall

Honda Insight, 1999

Toyota Prius I, 2002

Toyota Prius II, 2003

Boy. Building on the utility of the original *kei* car van and adding lifestyle content to it, this most quintessentially Japanese of all vehicle typologies evolved into the most visible member of Japan's mobile society. Japanese roads are nowadays populated by these small, upright motors, a majority of them in either white or, sometimes, one of the typically Asian metallic shades of a light pastel color—presumably catering to the female public. This little tall box is the true heir to the original Japanese car, being both narrow and tall. Acting as more of a miniaturized home nowadays, an environment that is just as intimate as it is social, the boxy shape only superficially appears to be yet another kind of uniform. With styles varying from retro to cartoon, modernist to sporty, these cars are just as diverse as the characters at the steering wheel, who may vary from the neat to the nasty, the humble to the snobby. One look inside also reveals a world of fancy accessories, hi-tech paraphernalia, or personal gear that characterizes the cabin as much as its inhabitant. The Tall Boy ought to be the ultimate form of intelligent individual mobility for the new millennium. But these facts notwithstanding, the new global markets are now being driven, in a very non-Japanese way, by anything but logical, if not outright irrational design decisions—which are no longer being taken in Japan, America, or Europe.

Suzuki Carry Van, 1969

Daihatsu Move Conte, 2008

Autech Nissan Dayz Rider, 2013

Suzuki Wagon R+, 1997

Daihatsu Move Latte, 2002

Honda N-ONE G·L Package, 2012

Toyota Duet, 1998

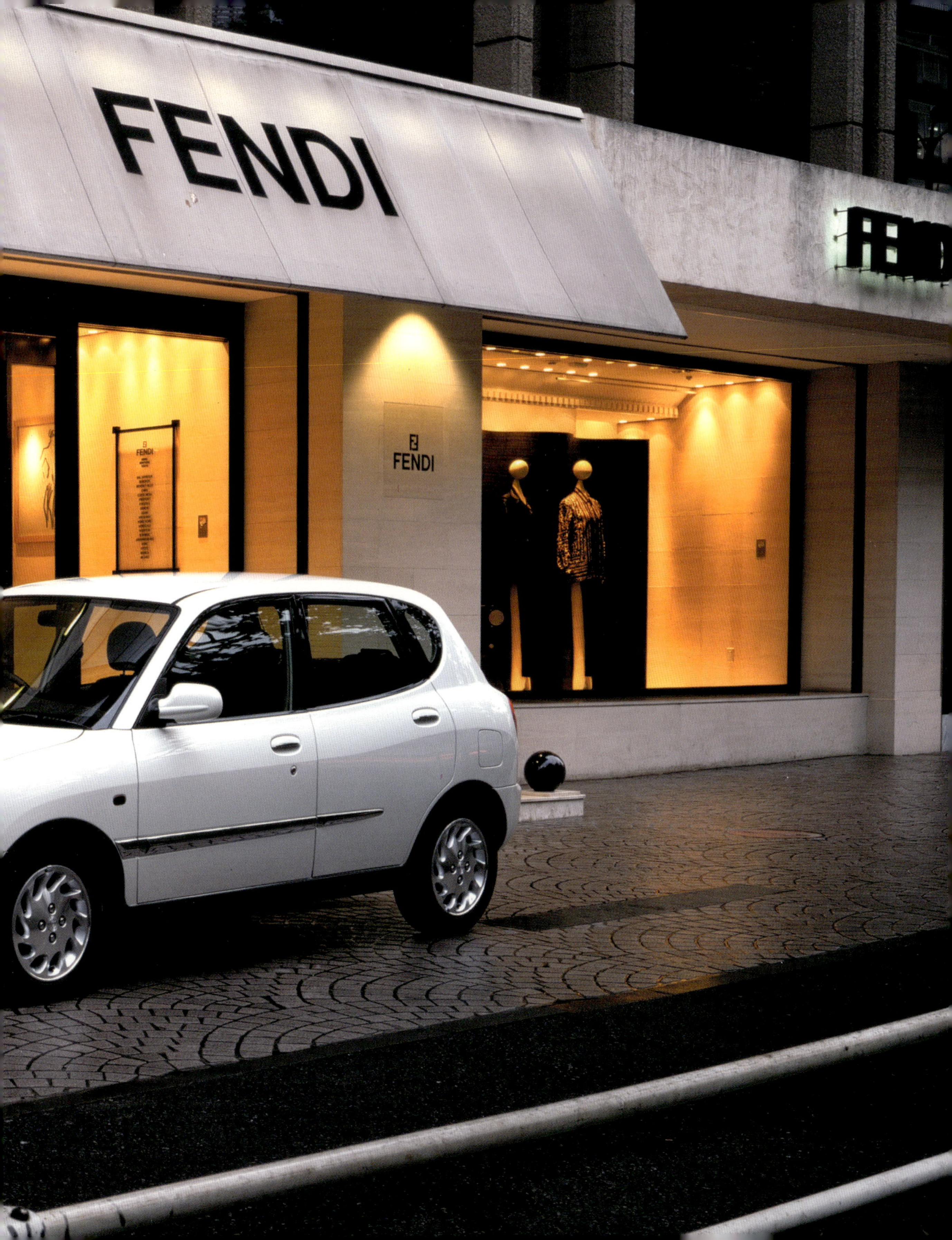
FENDI
FENDI

Mazda RX-8, 2003

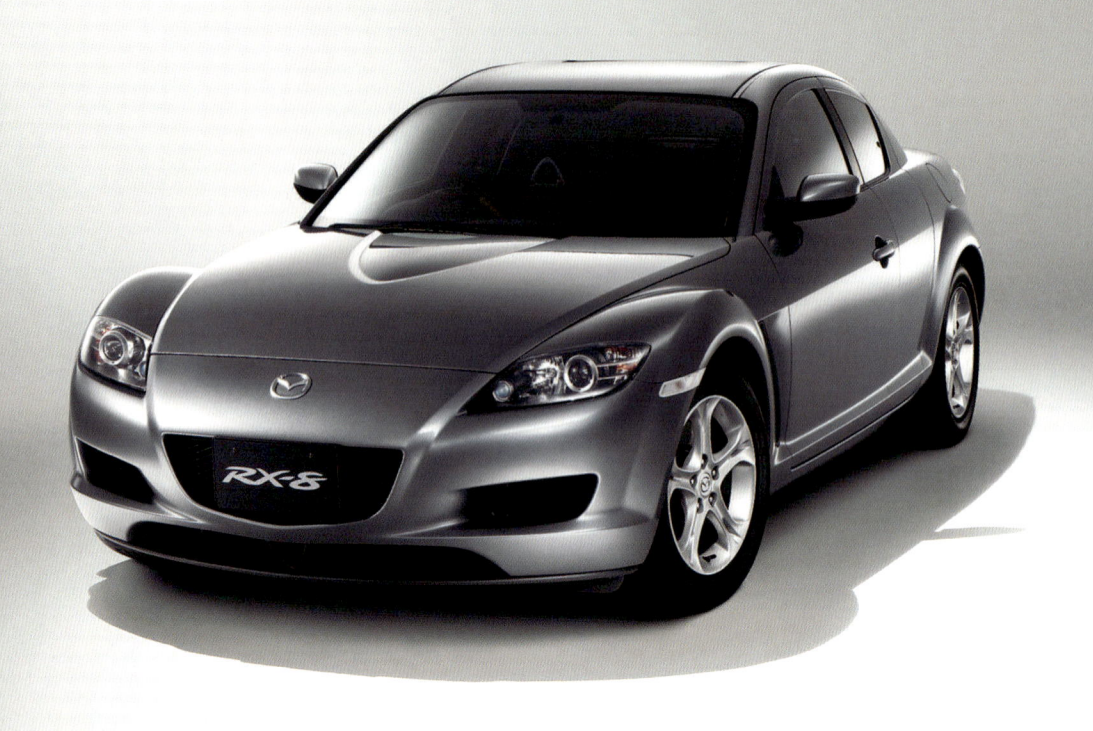

Nissan Primera, 2003

Nissan Fairlady Z, 2003

Toyota Mark X, 2006
Toyota Verossa, 2003

Lexus IS 300, 2003

Lexus IS 300 SportCross, 2003

LEXUS

It had been a clandestine project, pursued over the course of seven years, on different continents. So when Toyota's executives lifted the lid off their new Lexus LS 400 flagship, there had been little to prepare the competition in Stuttgart, Munich, Coventry, or Detroit for the shock that was in store for them. Here was a car, very closely modeled on the accepted best car in the world, Mercedes' S-Class, that bettered its role model in almost every regard—except, perhaps, for sheer performance. But then again, what is performance? No other brand has ever been ranked the #1 car maker for so long in J.D. Power's influential listing. So as the Europeans sniffed at the Lexus' bland, anodyne,

Lexus LS 460, 2006

somewhat derivative styling and antiseptic ambience, the US buyers could not have cared less. But if the LS was too Mercedes-like, the original GS—penned by Giugiaro and badged Toyota Aristo in Japan—carried a new message of status with speed, while the 1998 IS, with its sharply carved body, set new image rules for sporty sedan design.

Entering the new millennium, Lexus finally emancipated itself from the joint badging with Toyota and attacked Europe with a first genuine style of its own, the sophisticated L-Finesse. With increased self-confidence, the Mercedes-style grille was finally abandoned in favor of a new spindle grille, which pretends to protect Lexus' luxury image.

Mitsubishi Lancer, 2007

Nissan Stagea RX, 2004

Suzuki Wagon R, 1993

Suzuki Alto Lapin, 2002

TALL BOY

There are obvious differences between the motoring world in Japan and the rest of the planet. One such instance regards the triumph of the Tall Boy. Coinciding with the West's love affair with SUVs and crossover cars, the *kei* car has been reshaped in the image of the Suzuki Wagon R in 1993. Its taller roofline had the welcome side effect of lending the Wagon R a more brutish stance among the older, practical *kei* cars. Appealing to heart and mind alike, the Tall Boy look has since been adopted as the Japanese individual vehicle *par excellence*. In a country desperately missing private space, this miniaturized home-on-wheels appeals to the most primary of needs—intimacy—while providing a place to express one's own sociality. This rational build, coupled with a tatami-like footprint, results in attention not only being paid to the social space issue. Being available in an incredible array of styles, from cool to cute, from retro to spacy—the Tall Boy is as individual as people can be.

239

Honda That's, 2002

Honda Mobilio, 2002

Nissan Cube 3, 2003

Mitsubishi i, 2006

SCION

Scion is Toyota's solution to the shifting values of the American youth. A new brand aimed at adventurous and bold types, who would not like to be seen dead in a Camry. This special kind of customer embraces a less-is-more attitude, which means the Scions are not only sold in just one specification, but that they are actually physically small. Like a kind of grown up American *kei* car, the boxy xB openly displays its compact dimensions, ironizing them through its dwarfish Hot Rod stance. In 2004, the timing for such a reevaluation of what constitutes a cool car seems just about perfect: with record fuel prices and a growing appreciation of sustainability in the broadest sense, Scion's design, bold in character, but socially correct, appears to bring the consumption conflict to a positive end.

Scion xB, 2005

WiLL Vi, 2000

WILL

At the dawn of the millennium, with its home market share falling below 40%, Toyota considered itself out of touch with the younger Japanese buyers, who "possess clearly different values from those of previous generations, and who have begun to take a different course in consumer activities." In typically thorough fashion, Toyota decided to set up a dedicated marque-within-a-marque, targeted at that strange youth market, with an obvious bias towards female drivers. The fruit of this labor was WiLL, a brand name employed not just by Toyota, but by other Japanese consumer goods producers as well. The car itself was a daring mix of anti-automobile, big toy and fashion accessory. If WiLL and its range of post-modernist goods have been short-lived, then only because the advanced cross-branding enterprise appeared too early.

Mitsuoka Viewt, 1993

MITSUOKA

Susumu Mitsuoka understood the challenges Japanese car drivers longing for unique motoring had to face: imported cars were insanely expensive, the homegrown purveyors catered solely to conventional tastes and vintage cars were simply too impractical. To address this issue, Mitsuoka, connoisseur of British car design, came up with a striking formula, combining flamboyance with everyday practicality and reasonable value-for-money in the distinctive shape of the Mitsuoka Viewt. Attaching Jaguar Mk II-aping front and rear ends onto a Nissan March/Micra may seem peculiar to Western eyes, but in Japan, more than 10,000 car owners' taste buds have since been tickled by Mitsuoka's recipe for spicing up dreary everyday transport. This recipe was later on used to bring even bigger dreams to life, such as the Galue sedan and convertible or the Orochi super sports car.

Daihatsu Mira Cocoa, 2009

Daihatsu Copen, 2007

DAIHATSU

Albeit confined to offering the smallest of cars, Japan's oldest car manufacturer has time and again transcended the indigenous Japanese *kei* car market, for example at the 1963 Geneva Motor Show, where its Sport concept car—penned by Vignale of Turin, Italy—gave the European public a first taste of what Japanese car manufacturers were capable of. Years later, in 1980, the Daihatsu Cuore proved a hit with budget-conscious European drivers keen on basic, but reliable means of motoring. Under Toyota's wings, Daihatsu nurtured both its expertise and supremacy in the *kei* car sector back home in Japan, from the kiddish Mira to the aerobic Copen.

SSANGYONG

It hardly sounds like an act of derring-do when an unknown car maker hires a respected designer to spice up its model range. The world was therefore, following Italdesign's Mercedes-inspired Rexton, in for quite a surprise when SsangYong of South Korea began unveiling the fruit of its collaboration with former Aston Martin and Bentley designer, Ken Greenley, in 2004. For neither the Actyon SUVs nor the Rodius MPV looked like anything else on the road. Somehow, a British designer had created strongly Asian-flavored statements of visual flamboyance that were at odds with Western tastes. The critics were collectively gasping for air. But in the Actyon's case, its notoriety eventually turned into fame-of-sorts when BMW modeled its smash hit SUV coupé, the X6, in its image. And the Rodius will, quite simply, forever remain truly unique.

SsangYong Actyon, 2006

SsangYong Rexton, 2001

SsangYong Rodius, 2004

Autech Nissan Rafeet, 2007

Nissan Note, 2005

Toyota Estima, 2006

Toyota Hiace, 2004

Toyota Prius III, 2012

HYBRID SHAPE

A masterpiece of marketing through design, the hybrid shape has evolved into one of the defining trends in car styling of the new millennium. Starting with the first Honda Insight, perfected with the second generation of Toyota's Prius, a short, angled bonnet, coupled with a sloping roofline that ends in a Kamm tail spells out even to the casual onlooker that this is not your standard automobile—it does not feature the long bonnet, large wheels or squat stance that have been synonymous with power and prestige on roads all over the world for decades. Quite the contrary. Its basic shape and stance send out altogether different signals: "I am not excessively fast, I am not overpowered, I am not inconsiderately large, I am not here to boast about myself. I am sensible: look at my small bonnet, hiding a small engine. I am efficient: do you see my aerodynamically strong Kamm tail? I am a responsible car, and not some irrational penis substitute."

The hybrid shape has become a much more powerful symbol of hybrid propulsion than any graphic logo or even the noiselessness of hybrid cars in inner city traffic. As a result of its evocative power, it is being appropriated whenever a car needs to differentiate itself from the mainstream market as an ecologically responsible offering—whether it is powered by a traditional hybrid powertrain or hydrogen fuel cell is a secondary concern, a mere detail. The hybrid shape ensures that the global public receives the overall message.

Hy Breed   250

Honda CR-Z, 2010

Honda Insight, 2009

Honda Crosstour, 2009

Honda CR-Z, 2010

Acura ZDX, 2010

Toyota Corolla Altis, 2014

Nissan Dualis, 2006

CROSSOVER

Combining seemingly mutually exclusive attributes, be they agility and size or ruggedness and comfort, in order to create something that is above standard, is the name of the Crossover game. As supposedly nobody wants to drive an ordinary car, it is up to the alchemists in the design and marketing departments to achieve the impossible. Starting with a mixture of wagon, sports car, and truck in the shape of the Skyline Van, the Japanese have become among the most adroit of those wizards. Not only do they blend off-road appeal with decent on-road manners and usability for all the family—every now and then, they also come up with truly original, idiosyncratic concoctions like the Suzuki X-90, a dwarfish SUV for two (and two only), or the Honda Accord Crosstour, which aims at combining the best of the MPV, the estate car and the hatchback in one moderately sized package. As outlandish as some of these creations may appear, the mainstream success of the crossover is now beyond reproach. Nissan's Dualis, a small pseudo SUV, trumps the competition in the compact class by not appearing compact at all. Its wild brother, the eccentric Juke, melts the outrageous looks and impracticality of true exotica with the reliability of basic compact cars. The flavor of rebellion can thus appeal to even the most timid of rebels.

Nissan Juke, 2010

Nissan GT-R, (2007) 2013

NISSAN

In order to escape the small car stigma, what used to be Datsun until 1982 gradually evaporated into Nissan. The confusion only abated slowly, not helped by Nissan's hazy profile. On the one side, this truly was a "Mary-Ken" company, as far as manufacturing and marketing principles were concerned. Dating back to its Prince heritage, Nissan had also enjoyed some bragging rights, thanks to many achievements in the field of motor sports, as well as the pioneering adoption of turbo technology in the 1980s. On the other side, the new brand was too centred on its bread and butter Bluebird and March business to allow exotics like the dirty Safari, the benign Skyline or the legendary Fairlady Z—not to mention the outstanding world premiere that was the Prairie, the world's first MPV—to be considered on par with the mainstream. Nissan's metal melted during the very brand conscious '90s, a result of featureless white goods-on-wheels like the Pulsar or Avenir. Thankfully, Nissan's very own "lost decade" came to an end by the year 2000, when Carlos Ghosn and Shiro Nakamura took over as CEO and design director, respectively. These two cosmopolitans reawakened Nissan's international spirit, manifesting itself in a multicultural range of cars: The soft-edge Fairlady Z and Murano brought Nissan back on the design track, the crossover Dualis SUV on the business track, and the green Leaf—with its distinctly Japanese natural flavour—on the technology track.

Toyota FJ Cruiser, 2003

Honda Element, 2003

Mitsubishi L200 Double Cab, 2006

Hyundai Veloster, 2011

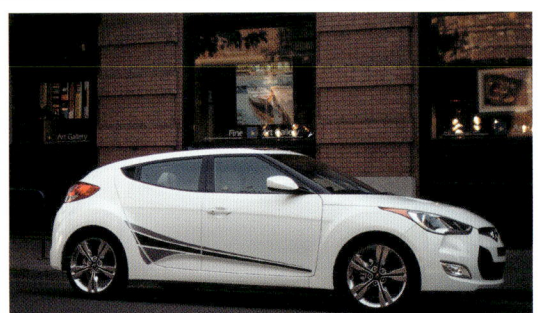

Scion IQ, 2012

Toyota IQ, 2012

Infiniti FX, 2009

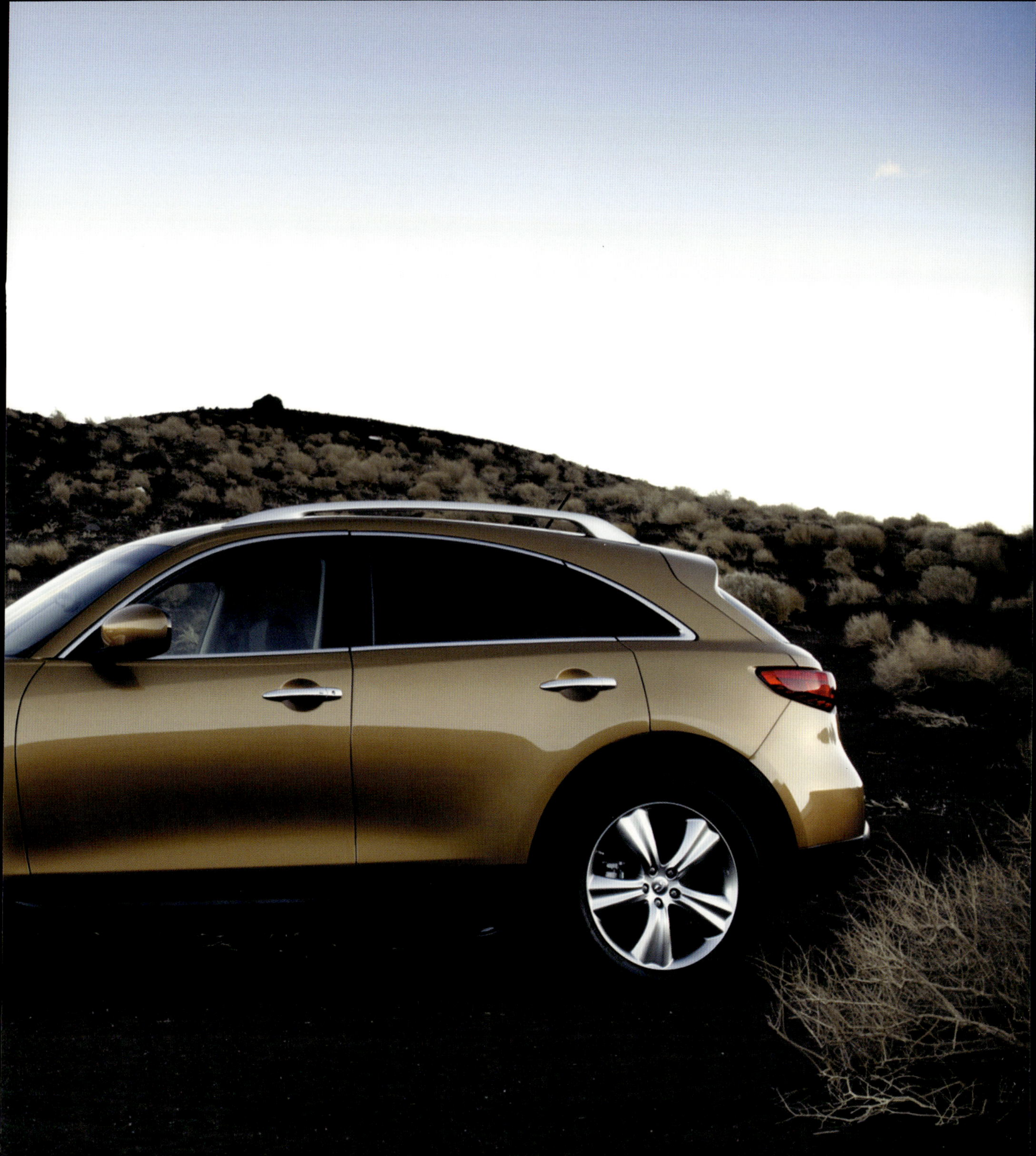

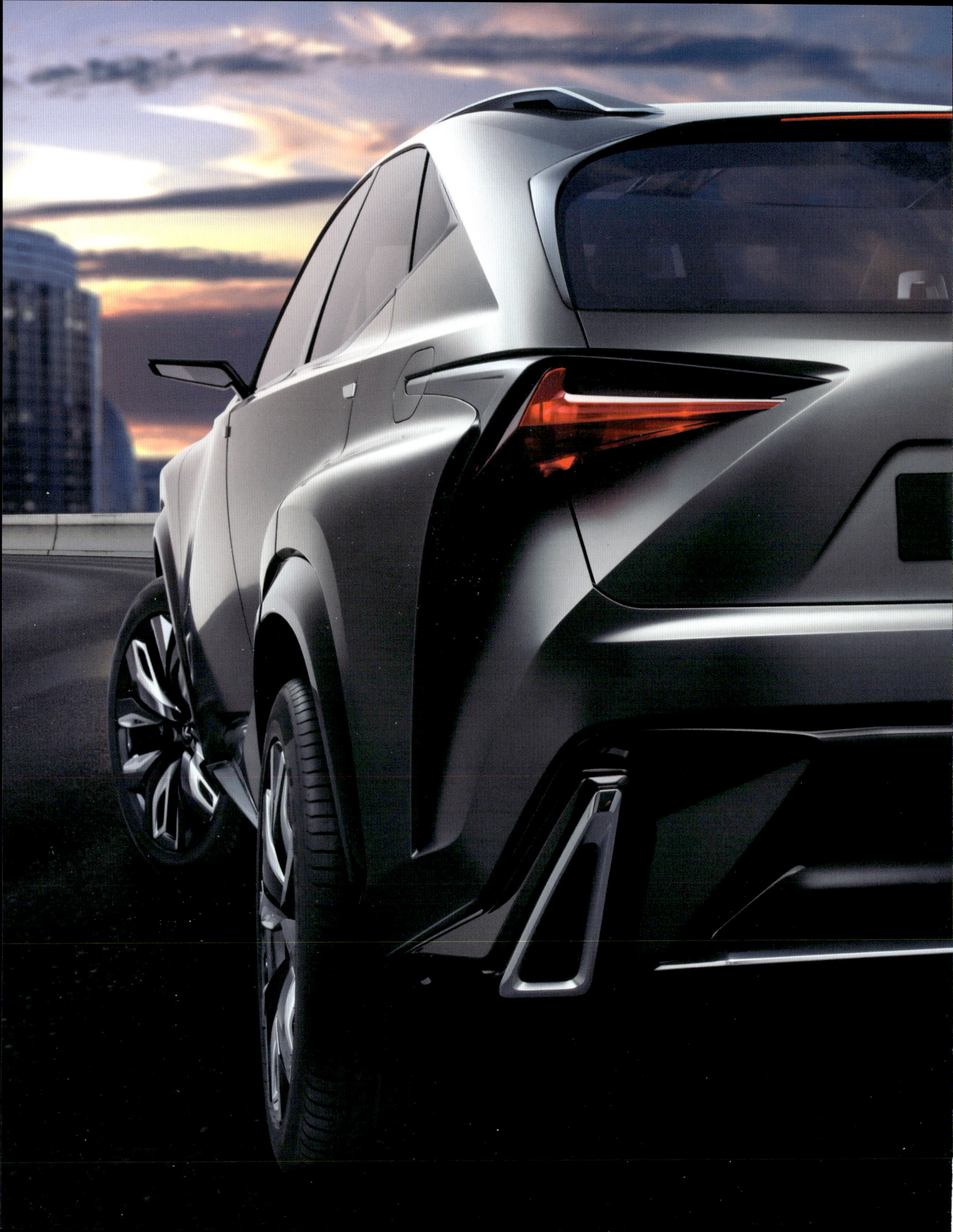

DRIVE OUT

Thanks to the pioneering adventures of the Japanese, automobility had become a global issue—and car design with it. In the meantime, all of East Asia had become a thoroughly different place. First with the help of Toyota, then General Motors, South Korea also went about entering the auto industry in the 1960s. Once independent, the South Koreans began moving swiftly, focusing on export markets and consistently upgrading their image: starting as a budget brand, developing into a mass market supplier and finally exhibiting premium ambitions. Reaching for the stars also seemed to be the brave aim of SsangYong, whose top-of-the-line Chairman—the name's political appeal being indisputable—was imitating both the Benz look and size since its inception in 1997.

Led by former Porsche chief engineer and later Aston Martin mastermind, Ulrich Bez, and repeatedly supported by Giugiaro in design matters, Daewoo was also enjoying its heyday in the '90s, becoming very popular abroad. In spite of their Italdesigned bodies, the boxy Hyundai Pony and Sonata's appearance had previously been just below average and unable to compete with either the Hondas or Renaults of the mid-'80s. But the soft shapes of the mid-'90s lent the Coupé—a very popular cheap sports car indeed—the Accent and the Santa Fe the trendy, if rather undistinguished vanilla look the Americans liked so much. And right in the middle of the 2000s, Hyundai finally unveiled its new face, which was not just meeting accepted standards of quality and style, but also conveyed a distinguished image. This would put the up-and-coming brand in the position of a main challenger of global players like Toyota and Volkswagen. However, Hyundai would rather place itself in the super sedan class of the individually badged Genesis and Equus, which are now properly competing against Mercedes-Benz. In 2006, Kia hired former Audi and VW design director, Peter Schreyer. With headquarters based in Frankfurt, the German was to become responsible for the design strategy of a genuinely global product palette. This lineup would also reach upwards by including the large and sporty K7

Lexus NX-LF, 2014

and K9 sedans—harboring not particularly latent anti-Audi ambitions. The image improvement in contrast to such whimsical South Korean models as the wannabe-Benz Kia Opirus was as conspicuous as the demonstration of improved build quality through an unlimited, seven-year warranty. Even though one may still smile at a candid YouTube video showing former Audi boss and Volkswagen Chairman, Martin Winterkorn, lamenting the superior quality of a Hyundai, there is no denying the fact that, within the shortest of timeframes, the South Koreans had moved upwards to become the world's fourth largest car manufacturer—right behind the Volkswagen Group. The South Korean success story also happened to be perfectly coinciding with the Japanese neighbor's weakness. In this context, business was but one fragment of this intricate love-hate relationship: through new TV formats and edgy movies, a new genre of South Korean lifestyle—not to mention the cool image of the sexy South Korean male (to whom a Latin boldness is attributed)—ended up fascinating the Japanese public, especially the female half. And as if to confirm the inner link between men and their cars, Japanese design followed the South Korean example and developed a bold and vividly imaginative car design language.

CHINA CHIC

Highlighting how sheer size can be uncontrollable, China's taking over as leading manufacturer and market proved itself to be a rather complicated venture. Except for the state limousine Hong Qi, which was hardly more than a promotional vehicle for Mao Zedong's "red flag" and is therefore still of a highly symbolic value today, China knew nothing about the automobile. In the wake of Deng Xiaoping's reforms, strongly centralized

SsangYong Chairman, 1997

Hyundai Pony, 1975

Hyundai Accent, 1994

Kia Opirus, 2003

Hyundai Sonata, 1988

Hyundai Coupé, 1996

political control led the four historically largest, state-owned manufacturers—charmingly named First Automotive Works, Second Automotive Works (later Dongfeng), Shanghai Automotive Industry Corporation, and Changan Automobile Group—to liaise with European and American partners. Oddly enough, rivals like Volkswagen and General Motors would find themselves partnering with the very same Chinese companies. No matter what the conditions though, the deal had to be accepted, as it meant the only possibility to access the appealing Chinese markets. The design implications of this development were hardly noteworthy: quick and dirty adaptations of older Western models to the Chinese taste, ideally in the shape of a midsize sedan—think BMW 3-series—stretched in order to bear Chairman Mao's flag. In spite of this political control, or maybe because of it, the automotive landscape in China reached conditions similar to those of the heydays of the automobile's pioneering age: in 2013, the top ten manufacturers shared 88.4% of the market for passenger cars, with the rest remaining in the hands of dozens of smaller competitors. Among these, imaginative domestic brand names, such as the nostalgic Great Wall, visionary Build Your Dreams, charming Chery, cheesy Geely, plain Brilliance, as well as reinvented British classics, MG and Roewe (for Rover), were to be found. In such a vast and rapidly growing market, foreign brands—German, Japanese, American, Korean, and French in order of importance—still count for around 60% of sales, while the share of Chinese brands actually declined for 2013. Export rates have been declining too, with 596,300 cars exported—peanuts compared to a domestic production of approximately 12 million cars and SUVs.

While China is cultivating her design consciousness, it appears as though Chinese branding and

Hong Qi, 1972

BMW 3 Li, 2014

design have yet to reach global standards. Then again, how could a bad copy of a BMW, a grotesque half Mercedes-Benz, half Renault creature, a pimped-up design relict in the image of a 1990s Rover, or the cute caricature sporting both the name and look of a (real) Panda ever meet the taste of the global public? Brilliance, whose skills had been trained through the production of stretch BMWs for China, went as far as hiring Pininfarina to facelift its Giugiaro-designed B6 sedan—odd in the same sense as asking Dior to refit an Armani dress would be—before finally hiring Pininfarina designer, Dimitri Vicedomini, to continue his work on location. Chery chose a similar approach and started a collaboration with former Pininfarina and Fiat designer, Enrico Fumia, who took the liberty to create one of the most extravagant, if not outright surreal objects ever put on wheels: the egg-shaped 2006 QQme, a kind of motorized Tamagotchi.

The average output of Chinese contemporary manufacturers seems to confirm an old rule whereby design quality emerges from the dialogue between designer and client. But when it comes to taste, no matter how well educated, the Chinese decision-makers' inevitably having missed half a century of consumption culture becomes all too apparent. This is the only way one can explain the unrestrained enthusiasm of Chinese drivers for their very first automobiles. If millions of utterly nondescript wannabe-Hong Qi notchbacks and sedans are being sold over the shop counter, regardless of their intrinsic design quality—just as refrigerators or TV sets would—then only so because the buyers know that this will not be their one and only, but one of many cars they may get to own in the future. Conversely, at the high end of the market, there is no hint of the museum-like admiration for the ultimate work of art. Instead, the carefully designed imported luxury car is

BYD S8, 2010

Geely Panda, 2009

Chery QQme, 2009

typically treated to the most individual finish. The Bentley Mulsanne for 2013 therefore comes in a "Seasons Collectors' Edition", featuring Asian-inspired color and trim of Golden Pine, Orchid, Bamboo, Chrysanthemum, and Plum Blossom, all with matching inlay marquetry by traditional Chinese artist, Lin Xi. The Gold one is limited to five, the four others—one for each season—to just ten specimen. Uniqueness is a highly regarded quality in a country of more than a billion people, obviously.

Be they shiny, matte or glittering—or any combination of the three—the Western beauties crowding the streets are seen wearing gold, pink, purple, or lime green. To them, nothing is either too kitschy or too cool. Fashion patterns are just as trendy as glow-in-the-dark effects over matte black lining, which strikingly extracts the complexity of contemporary car design. A theatrical use of the automobile fetish corresponds to this costume play. The website carnewschina.com lists giant gatherings of hundreds of super sports cars, as well as the most absurd accounts of roadside luxury car crashes, climaxing with something uniquely Chinese: "Super Car Weddings", as part of which a dozen black Rolls-Royce Phantoms, all "dressed up with fake plastic flowers" are depicted as they are being followed by a bunch of "extremely common" red Ferraris, creating the most exquisitely designed traffic jams. No matter how the concerned European likes to judge this stance: China seems to be as indigent as it is ingenious, and beautifully free to create a new style of automotive conspicuous consumption.

Among the plethora of odd, funny, or simply unfortunate regular models, few brands could be described as standing above the crowds and likely to be setting the standard for a globally compatible Chinese design quality. The Denza, a joint venture between Daimler and Build Your Dreams,

Brilliance BS6, 2004

Roewe 750, 2006

Shuanghuan SCEO, 2007

whose flowing notchback design places it just between Chinese and German style, aims at the luxury electric vehicle market. Directed by Mini's former design chief, Gert Hildebrand, Qoros pioneered the integration of Western design within a purely Chinese organization, and now finds itself able to withstand the global design competition's scrutiny at the Geneva Motor Show.

ASIAN STYLE

Be it of Japanese, South Korean, or Chinese origin—a new, genuinely Asian style has unquestionably been assuming shape since the 2010s. While generalizing is difficult, a joint evolution would not be all that surprising, as the three countries—in spite of the many different attempts at claiming superiority—are rooted in the very same cultural heritage. There are, above all, three common style elements that must be present in contemporary Asian car design: calligraphy, the dragon, and the pagoda. Albeit different in style, Asian characters positively reject the geometrical construction of the Roman alphabet. This rigidity of Western block capitals of Greek heritage had influenced classic and modernist architecture, as well as fashion and finally car design later on—from the '60s *trapèze* line to the '80s box. Following this logic, the fluidity of Asian calligraphy, although ideally inscribed within a square, must influence the dynamic flow, the crisp intersections and the brusque interruptions of the automobile's lines—the new Infiniti's flows being just as good an example for this as the Equus' dynamic or the Lexus LF-NX's kaleidoscopic sculpting. A strong mythological figure both in China and Japan, the dragon's expressive tension, its bulky eyes and amazing face may be discovered not only in the visual accentuation of the front end compared to the rest of the body, but in the rather theatrical

Denza NEV, 2012

BYD Qing, 2014

Qoros 3, 2014

facial expression itself—as seen on the Lexus spindle grill or its variation by Infiniti. The pagoda, on the other hand, with its upward facing architecture, adds the vertical dynamic element the Western skyscraper dearly misses and which serves the aesthetic of both the Tall Boy and the regular SUV so well. If it is to be considered a form of Qing baroque, then the pagoda differs from Western baroque in that the latter is convex, while the former is eminently concave—a principle easily found in new Asian cars' surfaces and style (and to be spotted in the latest Infiniti side window). All this may seem odd to a Western public accustomed to classic urban patterns, but to understand the new Asian car design, one has to see the cars in their natural environment: the Chinese megacity, or even just Seoul—Tokyo being too classic a metropolis. In front of such gigantic buildings, amid extra large carriageways, the automobile requires a larger size, a bolder stance, and a more expressive style, simply to be noticed. It is clearly too early to state whether today's Asian style will set an enduring trend. The new role of Asia as a global design motor is not to be misunderstood though. Since China has become the world's largest market, no manufacturer can ignore the needs, wishes, and dreams of the former Celestial Empire. As the South Korean and Japanese manufacturers are being confronted with the necessity to adapt a genuinely Asian-inspired design language, the Western school has to face the Eastern design challenge, too. There is one example that says it all: with the animalistic stance of a dragon, the fluid lines of calligraphy, and a baroquely decorative style, the 2013 Mercedes-Benz S-Class, this most German of all German cars, appears to have been designed with the Chinese customer in mind above everyone else.

Kinkaku-ji, Kyoto, 1397

Calligraphy

Dragon

Autech Nissan Dayz Roox Rider, 2013

Nissan Leaf, 2010

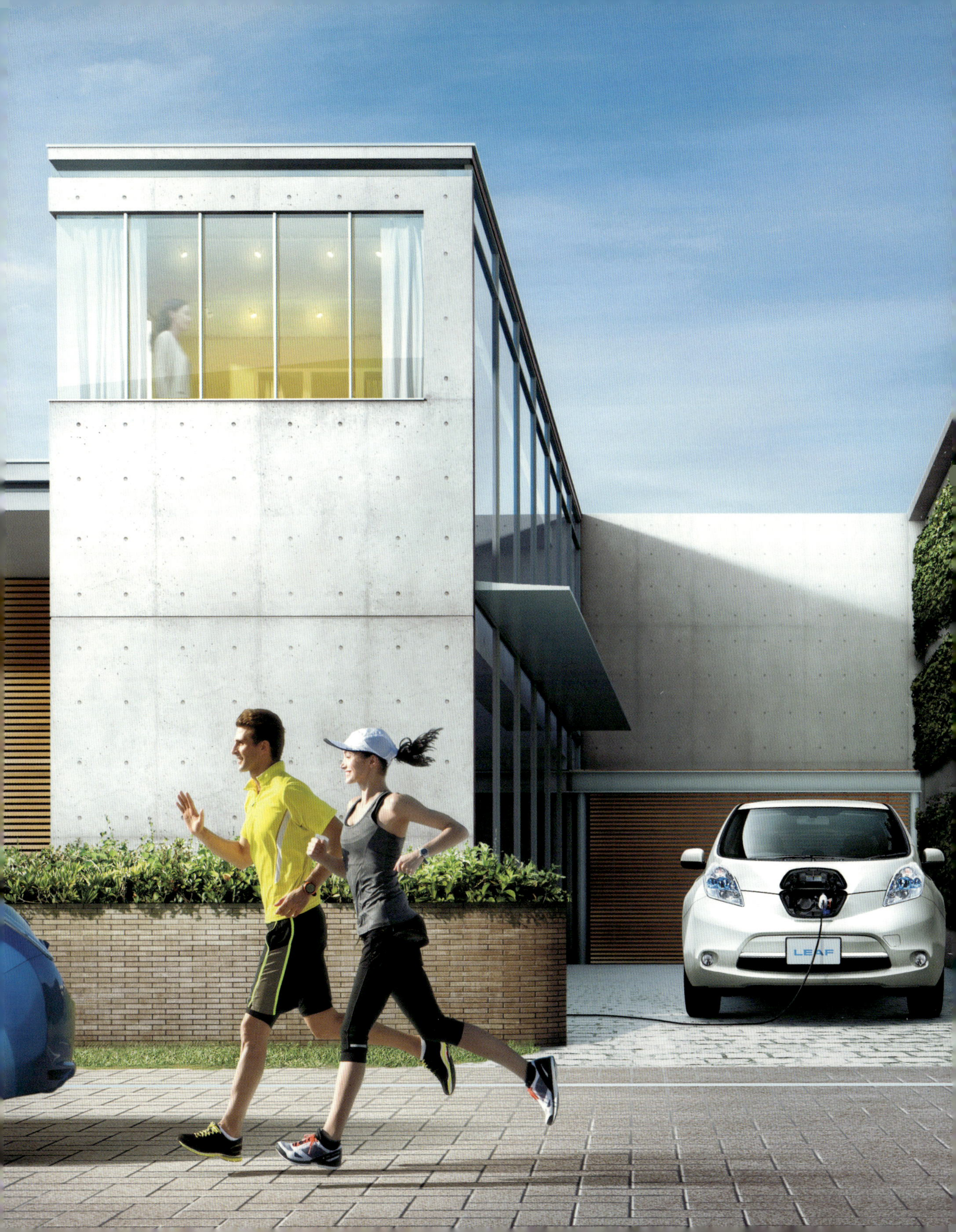
LEAF

Kia Rio sedan, 2013

Kia Sedona, 2006

Kia Rio, 2011

Kia Sorento, 2009

KIA Optima, 2010

KIA

The year is 1997. Kia, producer of a range of, at best, average cars selling only on low price, is declaring bankruptcy amidst the turmoil of the Asian financial crisis. It survived with Mercedes-Benz-aping concoctions like the Opirus and the Carens—which were too kitschy to be true. A mere 20 years later, the situation presents itself in an altogether different light. Kia is a thriving business, selling cars that are actually desirable—and not just so to the Korean family man, but to people all over the globe. This almost magical change of fortunes is not only

Kia Forte, 2009

Kia Forte Koup, 2009

Kia Forte 5, 2011

Kia Soul, 2010

Kia Sportage, 2010

due to new parent Hyundai's commitment—it is the result of an exemplary case of brand repositioning. Among the most cunning moves of this master plan was the hiring of respected former Audi and Volkswagen designer, Peter Schreyer, in 2006. He turned a mostly derivative and incoherent range of automobiles into an attractive product portfolio, easily recognizable thanks to its "tiger nose." Known in Europe as a small car maker, Kia offers executive and luxury saloons in Asia and the US that aim at competing with BMW—or did anybody say Audi?

Drive Out   276

Kia Soul, 2013

Toyota GT 86, 2013

Mazda Biante, 2008

Honda Civic Type S, 2007

279

Honda Fit Hybrid, 2013

Toyota Aqua G Sports, 2013

Hyundai Genesis coupé, 2013

HYUNDAI

Offspring of the mighty Hyundai *chaebol*, the Hyundai Motor Company's first car is rightly called Pony—styled by Giugiaro for the not-so-cool Korean driver, it is far from a race horse. Despite Giugiaro's later models almost meeting the master's standards, the conquest of foreign markets was proving to be far from plain sailing: in the US, and after a sensational first year of sales—in fact the best market entry ever recorded at that point—Hyundai quickly became synonymous with cheap engineering and lousy build quality. Over the course of the 1990s, the laughing stock was gradually being taken seriously. The soft Coupé was ranked bestselling sports car in Italy. And come the dawn of the new millennium, only fools would laugh at the South Koreans anymore, for their products were now not just very reasonably priced, but also more fashionable. When Hyundai became the main sponsor of the 2006 Soccer World Cup in Germany, even the notoriously difficult European market took note and bought Korean. This exposure raised brand awareness and, soon after, prices were raised, too—Hyundai, after all, was not selling shoddy also-rans anymore, but competitive products of sophisticated Asian styling and a build quality that would impress even the Teutons. With this upmarket push still in full swing, helped by a coherent, global design language, Hyundai projects onto its styling the ambition of being a Mercedes-Benz of Asian provenance.

Hyundai Elantra, 2010

Toyota Auris, 2012

Toyota Avensis, 2011

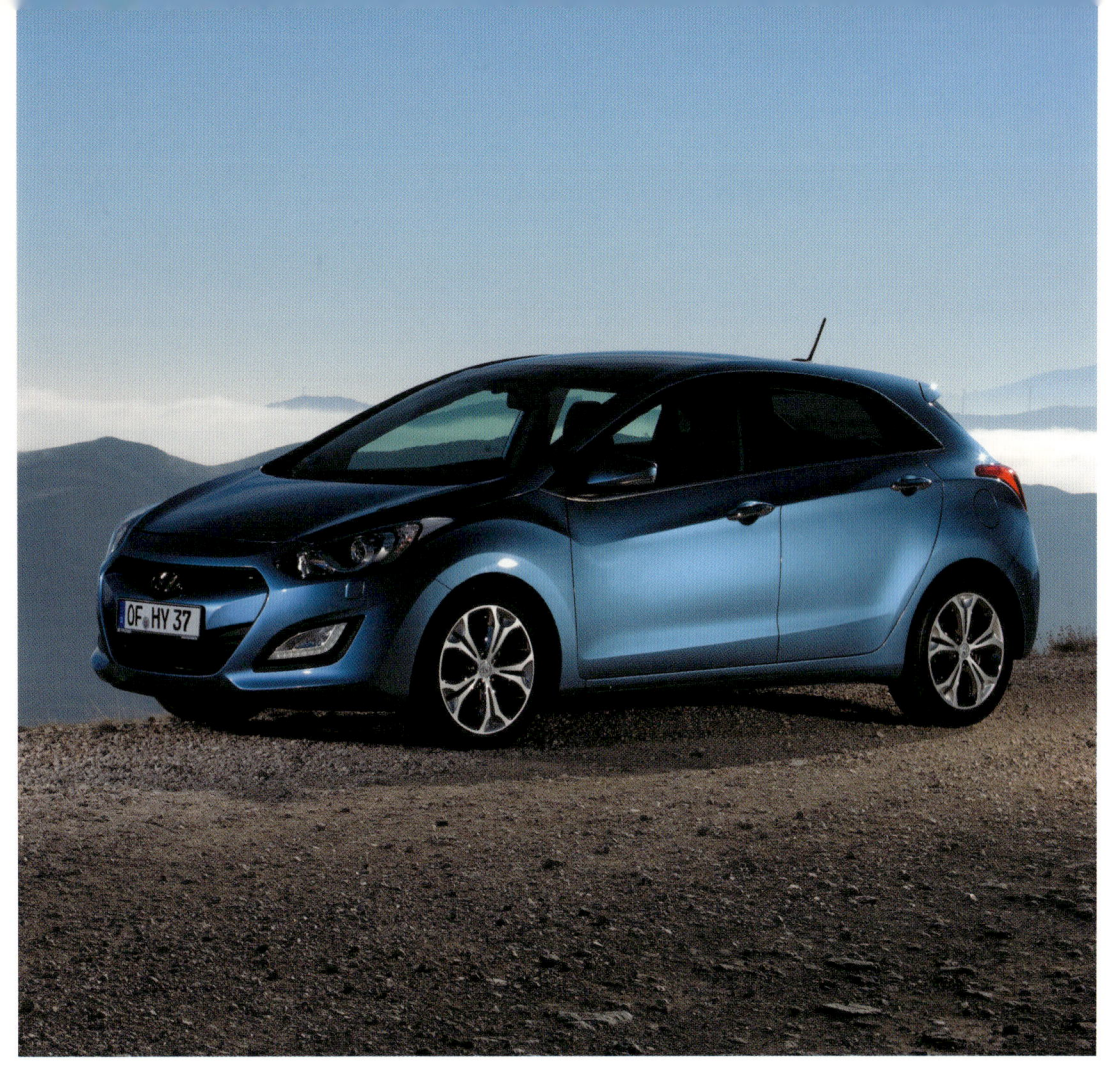

Hyundai i30, 2012

Hyundai i40 Wagon, 2012

Lexus GS 300h, 2013

Infiniti Q50, 2013

INFINITI

Beginning with a would-be Jaguar XJ—the original Q45—Infiniti initially set itself apart through a rather erratic product strategy. The fact that Infiniti was selling expensive Nissans was about the best definition of the brand most could agree upon. But then, Nissan's new boss, Carlos Ghosn, ordered a thorough repositioning of the brand. This obviously called for a clearly defined new image, with styling to match—which Nissan's chief designer, Shiro Nakamura, duly delivered, starting with the tense, muscular lines of the 2003 FX45 SUV—the prototype of the hot, sporty SUV. Among the usual

Infiniti QX60, 2014

marketing babble accompanying the relaunch, the term *adeyaka* stood out: meaning luster and gloss, it sums up the modern Infiniti range rather well. For these are distinctly Asian cars with a strong oriental flavor. Similar to Lexus' spindle, Infiniti's pagoda grill is as uniquely Asian as a car face can get.

This bulbous, sometimes borderline surreal appearance does not intend to cater to European aesthetics. In that sense, the former also-ran is all of a sudden the leader of the Japanese premium herd.

Equus, 2013

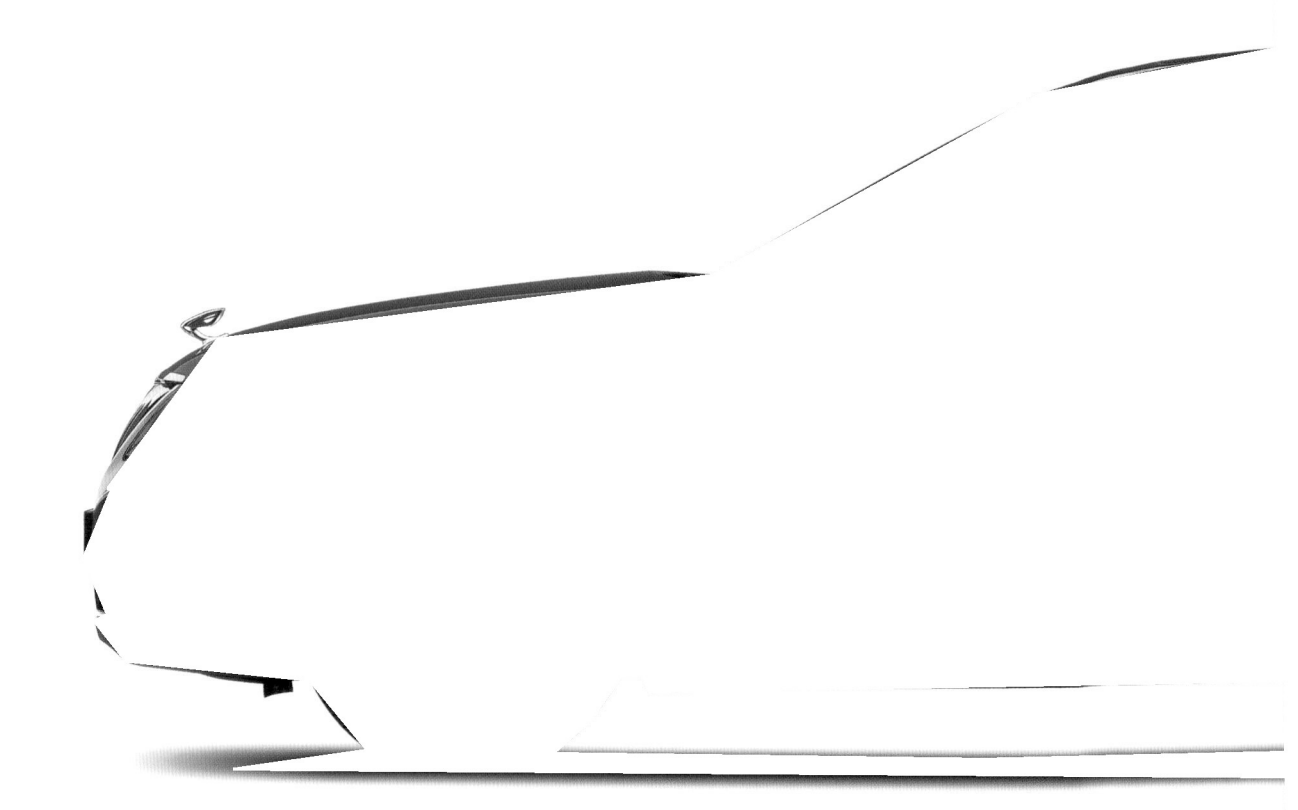

EQUUS

Here is a premium Korean brand whose size put the gold standard of the class, Mercedes' S-Class, in its shadow. More importantly, its bespoke engineering serves as forceful reminders that the days when Hyundai had to fall back on Mitsubishi for technology were over. Yet the bridging of gaps is only half the story: this power horse is more than just a well-bred epigone, establishing standards of its own, most obviously through its self-confident, if not too expressive stance. Nobody expects a shrinking violet in this demanding market, yet Hyundai ups the ante by lending the Equus the proportions and appearance of a state limousine of Asian heritage. This goes to highlight the special challenge set by Asia's megacities: it takes both size and a self-conscious dose of ornamentation to get recognized on multi-lane roads at the feet of the most gigantic buildings. Unlike Japan's visually humble Toyota Century, the Korean plutocrat's means of transport is intent on catering to this desire with no holds barred.

Drive Out 292

Kia K9, 2012

Toyota Crown Athlete, 2012

Toyota Harrier Hybrid, 2014

Autech Nissan Elgrand Rider, 2010

Nissan Serena, 2011

Mazda Axela, 2013

Toyota Vellfire, 2011

Nissan Teana, 2014

Qoros 3, 2013

QOROS

After the world has been selling its automobiles to China, with Qoros, China seems ready to reciprocate. This Chinese–Israeli consortium's product is being developed in Austria by experienced European engineers and styled under the auspices of German designer Gert Hildebrand—formerly in charge of Mini's design—but built in and for China. The Qoros 3, the outcome of this diligent undertaking, is an unquestionably competent piece of design that would not look out of place in either Shanghai, Hanover or Istanbul. Its inconspicuous, instant respectability distracts from the more significant fact that the Qoros is the ultimate world car. That it also raises Chinese car design onto a globally competitive level seems almost marginal in that context.

Lexus IS, 2013

Acura RLX, 2014

REGISTER

ACURA: Integra 15, *188*, 189, Legend 178, *188*, 188, ZDX 252, RLX 299 — AUTOZAM: Carol 175, 192, Revue 179, *199*, AZ-1 *190*, 191 — BMW: 3 *267*, 267 — BRILLIANCE: B6 *268*, 269 — BYD: S8 268, Qing 270 — CHERY: QQme 268, *268* — DAEWOO: Lanos *205*, 205, Matiz *205*, 205, Nubira 205 — DAIHATSU: Compagno *25*, 25, Charade *138*, 138, Move 227, Mira 244, *244*, Copen 244, *244* — DATSUN/NISSAN: Exa *14*, 14, *142*, 1000 20, *21*, PL110 *21*, Fairlady (Z) 21, *53*, *61*, 101, 102, *102*, 116, 116, 117, 118, 119, *123*, 181, *181*, *193*, 222, 231, *256*, Cedric 24, 24, 25, 34, 35, *53*, 73, *97*, 138, 184, 186, Bluebird 53, *54*, 54, 57, 60, 61, *61*, 72, *95*, 102, *256*, Sunny 54, 54, 55, 77, President 55, 68, 69, *177*, Skyline 56, 56, 70, 71, 78-79, 80, 81, 102, 114, 115, 157, 174, 256, Laurel 56, *174*, Cherry 57, 72, 75, 76, Murano 69, *222*, 222, *257*, Violet 75, 78, 620 Cab Truck 89, Silvia *99*, 100, *101*, 130, 131, 142, R381 115, Leopard 134, 144-145, *174*, 174, *181*, 181, CUE-X *137*, *143*, 143, Pulsar *138*, 158, 161, *257*, Prairie 139, 166, *256*, Safari 142, 167, March 160, *179*, *181*, *193*, 193, 194, 195, *222*, 224, *243*, Largo 163, Cefiro 170-171, Cima 176, *177*, 184-185, Gloria 177, *178*, Be-1 *178*, *179*, 179, 194, Pao *179*, 195, S-Cargo *179*, 194 Figaro *179*, 194, *195*, Autech March Bolero *179*, 195, 300 ZX *181*, 181, Avenir *181*, 181, Autech March Tango 195, Serena 209, 294, Cube 3 *224*, 240, Rasheen *224*, 225, Dualis *225*, 254, Juke *225*, 225, 255, Autech Dayz Rider 227, Primera 231, Stagea 237, Autech Rafeet 246, Note 246, GT-R 256-257, Leaf *257*, 272-273, Autech Dayz Roox Rider 271, Autech Elgrand Rider 293, Teana 295 — DENZA: *269*, 270 — EFINI: RX-7 198 — EQUUS: *265*, 290-291 — EUNOS: Roadster *14*, *149*, 180, 197, Cosmo *196*, 196, 199, FIAT: 124 *54*, 54 — GEELY: Panda *268*, 268 — HINO: Contessa 24, 24, 32, 33, *33* — HONDA: NSX *14*, 14, 165, Accord 15, 15, *141*, 164, *165*, Z *23*, *103*, 103, 121, 122, 123, N 360 *38*, 40, *220*, Civic 56, 57, *141*, 141, *165*, 166, *219*, 278, 289, 1300 74, S 360-800 *97*, 97, *105*, 108, *121*, Prelude 138, 141, 164, City *139*, 139, 160, Motocompo *139*, 139, Ballade Sports CR-X *141*, 141, 165, Vigor *141*, *174*, 174, Acty 163, Today *178*, 179, Beat *190*, 191, FCX Clarity 214, *226*, S2000 220, *220*, N-ONE *220*, 227, Hondajet 222, *222*, HR-V *225*, 225, Crossroad *225*, 225, Insight *226*, 226, 249, 250 CR-Z *226*, 250, 251, That's 239, Mobilio 239, Crosstour 250, Element 259, Fit 279 — HONG QI: *266*, 267 — HYUNDAI: Coupé 211, *265*, 266, Veloster 260, Pony *265*, 266, *280*, Sonata *265*, 266, Accent *265*, 266, Genesis *265*, 280, Elantra 281, i30 283, i40 283 — INFINITI: Q45 *177*, 185, *286*, FX 262-263, *286*, Q50 285, QX60 286-287 — ISUZU: Hillman Minx 10, *20*, Florian 37, Bellett 47, *113*, 113, 117 Coupé *102*, 112, *113*, Piazza 113, *143*, 143 — ITALDESIGN: Megagamma 138, *139* — KIA: K9 *266*, 292, Opirus *266*, 266, *274*, Optima 274, Sorento 274, Rio 274, Sedona 274, Forte 275, Soul 275, 276, Sportage 275 — LEXUS:

ES 15, **LS** *178*, 178, 234-235, **SC** *181*, 182-183, **IS** *220*, 233, 298, **LFA** 221, **GS** *235*, 284, **NX-LF** 264, 270 — **MAZDA: R360** *23*, 39, **P360 Carol** 23, **Luce** *25*, 42-43, 78, 128, 150, 185, **Familia** 36, 46, *104*, 200, **Cosmo** 94, 99, *101*, 106-107, 129, 151, **Capella** *104*, 126-127, *199*, **Savanna RX-7** *104*, 104, 132-133, 174, *181*, **626** *136*, 148, 208, **323** *136*, 146, 160, *199*, **MX-5 (Miata)** *179*, **MX-6** 181, **Xedos 6** *181*, 199, **5** *199*, 223, **Roadster** 200, 220, *224*, 224, **Millenia** 201, **RX-8** 230, **Biante** 278, **Axela** 294 — **MITSUBISHI: Model A** *9*, 9, **500** *22*, 24, **Minica** *38*, 38, 41, **Colt** 44, 45, *85*, *136*, 147, **Debonair** *55*, 58-59, *138*, 138, **Lancer** 82, 83, 236, **Galant** 84, 85, *136*, 149, 150, **Pajero** *85*, *142*, 142, 167, **Space Wagon** *85*, 166, **Delica** 86, **Celeste** 87, **Dangan** *138*, **Sapporo** 149, **i** 240, **L200** 259 — **MITSUOKA: Viewt** 243, *243*, **Galue** *243*, **Orochi** *243* — **MUJI: Car 1000** *222* — **PRINCE: Skyline** 25, 28, 29, *29*, 30, **Gloria** *29*, *55*, 55, **1900 Sprint** 31, *99* — **QOROS: 3** 270, 296-297 — **ROEWE: 750** 269 — **SCION: xB** *241*, 241, **IQ** 261 — **SHUANGHUAN: SCEO** 269 — **SSANGYONG: Actyon** 245, *245*, **Rexton** 245, *245*, **Rodius** 245, *245*, **Chairman** *265*, *266*, 266, 267 — **SUBARU: Alcyone** *14*, 14, *181*, *204*, 204, **360** *22*, 22, 39, *97*, **1000** 37, **Leone** *104*, 105, 124, **R-2** 122, 123, **Domingo** 163, **Legacy** 174, **Vivio** 192, **Impreza** *204*, 204 — **SUZUKI: Suzulight** *22*, 22, **Fronte** 22, 40, *104*, 123, *123*, **Carry Van** 22, 227, **Cappuccino** *23*, *190*, 190, **Jimny** *104*, 105, *123*, 123, 202, **SJ** *142*, 142, **Twin** 193, **Wagon R**, *202*, 227, 238, **Escudo** *202*, 203, **X-90** 203, 294, **Alto Lapin** 238 — **TAKURI: Type 3** *8*, 9 — **TOYODA: AA** 9, *10* — **TOYOTA: (Toyopet) SA** *10*, 20, **(Toyopet) Crown** *10*, 11, *21*, 21, *53*, *55*, 55, 56, 64, *65*, 67, *97*, 186, 187, 218, *220*, 292, **Corolla** 12, 13, *13*, *54*, 54, *65*, 65, *219*, *222*, 222, 253, **Bb** 14, **Camry** 15, *15*, *54*, 150, **Prius** 15, *226*, 226, 248-249, **(Toyopet) Corona** 18, *24*, 24, *53*, *54*, 54, 62, 184, **Publica** *24*, 26-27, 48-49, *97*, 97, **Century** *55*, 66-67, 291, **Corona Mark II** 63, *224*, **2000 GT** 65, *98*, 98, 110-111, *111*, **Hi-Lux**, 88, *104*, 105, 124, *142*, 142, **Celica** 90, 92-93, 151, 152, 153, 172, *180*, 180, *222*, 222, **Chaser** 91, 206, **800 Sports** *97*, 109, **Land Cruiser** *104*, 125, *142*, *168*, 168-169, 219, 288, **Starlet** *136*, 146, 147, **Sprinter Trueno** 140, **4Runner** *142*, **Sprinter Carib** *142*, 166, **Soarer** 142, 154-155, *181*, **MR-2**, 159, *181*, 181, *222*, 222, **Carina** 161, **Mini Ace** *162*, **HiAce** 162, 247, **Lite Ace** *162*, **Town Ace** *162*, **Master Ace** *162*, 162, **Celsior** *178*, **Aristo** *178*, 178, *235*, **Curren** 207, **RAV4** 207, *222*, *225*, **Sprinter Marino** 208, **Estima** 209, 247, **Supra** 210, **Sera** 212-213, *222*, **FJ Cruiser** 219, 258, **Origin** 218, *220*, **Altezza** 220, *220*, **Auris** 222, *224*, 224, 282, **Avensis** *222*, 282, **Mark X** *224*, 224, *225*, 232, **Fun Cargo** *224*, 225, **Probox** *224*, 225, **Vitz** 224, **Harrier Hybrid** *225*, 293, **Duet** 228-229, **Verossa** 232, **IQ** 261, **GT 86** 277, **Aqua** 279, **Vellfire** 295 — **TRIUMPH: Spitfire 1500** *180*, 180 — **WiLL: Vi** *195*, *222*, *242*, 242 ∎

CREDITS

© Wikimedia Commons 8(l), 96(r), 102(r), 269(tl-bl-m) — © National Museum of the US Air Force 20(tl) — © Tezuka Productions 23(l) — © Image Source/Corbis 6 — © Mr. Folchini 8(r) — © Goodbrands Institute 9(tl), 16-17, 102(r), 136(l), 265(l),303 — © Mitsubishi Motors Corporation 9(bl), 22(br), 38, 41, 44, 45, 58-59, 82-87, 147(l), 149, 166(bm-br), 236, 240(b), 258(b) — © Toyota Motor Corporation 9(r), 11, 12, 13, 15(l-tm-bm), 18, 20(bl), 21(tr-br), 24(bl), 26-27, 48-49, 54(tm-br), 55(l-br), 56(tl), 62-67, 88, 90-93, 97(tl), 98, 105(tr), 109, 110-111, 124(b), 125, 140, 142(mb), 146(b), 147(b), 150(b), 151(b), 152-153, 154-155, 159(r), 161(t), 162, 166(bl), 168-169, 172, 178(bl-r), 180(r), 181(tm), 182-183, 184(br), 186(b), 187, 206, 207, 208(t), 209(t), 210, 212-213, 218, 219, 220(r), 221, 222(tm-bm-br), 224(bl-bm-br), 225(tl-br), 226(bl-r), 228-229, 232-235, 241, 242, 247, 248, 252, 255, 259, 264, 277, 279(b), 282, 284, 288, 292(b), 293(t), 295(t), 298 — © Isuzu Motors 10, 37(b), 47, 112, 113, 143(l) — © Nissan Motor Company 14(tl), 20(r), 21 (l), 24(tl), 25(r), 28-31, 34, 35, 50, 52, 53, 54(bl-bm-tr), 55(tr), 56(bl-r), 57(tr-br), 60, 61, 68-73, 75(tr-br), 76-81, 89, 100, 101, 102 (tl-bl), 114-119, 130, 131, 134, 137(l), 139(l), 142(tl-ml), 143(tr-br), 144-145, 158, 160(bl), 161(br), 163(b), 167(tm-tr), 170-171, 174(tr-r), 176, 177, 179(br), 181(l-bm-br), 184(t-bl), 185(t-br), 186(t), 193(t), 194-195, 209(b), 222(tr), 224(tr), 225(bl-tm), 227(tr), 231, 253, 254, 256-257, 262-263, 271(r), 272-273, 285-287, 293(b), 294(t), 295(b) — © Fuji Heavy Industries 14(bl), 22(l), 37(t), 39(t), 105(l), 122(b), 124(t), 163(m), 174(bl), 192(b), 204, 237, 240(t), 246 — © Honda Motor Co. 14(r), 15(tr-br), 40(b), 57(l), 74, 97(br-l), 103(r), 108, 120, 121, 122(t), 139(tr-br), 141, 160(bm), 163(t), 164, 165, 166(tl), 174(bm), 178(tl), 179(tr), 187, 188, 191(b), 214, 220(bl), 222(l), 225(bm-tr), 227(br), 239(t-b), 249-251, 258(t), 278(b), 279(t), 289 — © Suzuki Motor Corporation 22(tm-bm-br), 40 (t-m), 105(br), 123, 142(tr), 190, 193(b), 202, 203, 227(tl-bl), 238(t-m), 299 — Original marketing collateral (excerpt) 24(r), 25(tl-bl), 103(bl), 104(l), 136(m-r), 138(tl-bl) — © Hino Motors 32, 33 — © Mazda Motor Corporation 36, 39(b), 42-43, 46, 94, 99, 14(r), 106-107, 126-127, 128, 129, 132-133, 146(t), 148, 150(t), 151(t), 160(t) , 174(bm), 175(br), 179(l), 180(l), 181(tr), 184(br), 1919(t), 192(t), 196-201, 208(b), 220(tl), 223, 224(tr-tm), 226(tl), 230, 278(t), 294(b) — © Fiat Chrysler Automobiles 54(tl) — © Sony Corporation 96(tl-bl), 103(tl), 137(tr-br), 216 — © Italdesign Giugiaro 138(r) — © Dino Dalle Carbonare 142(bl), 156-157 — © Olympus Corporation 175(tr), 217 — © Sanrio Co. 175(l) — © Daewoo Motors 205 — © Hyundai Motor Company 211, 260, 266(tm-bm-tr-br), 280, 281, 283, 290-291 — © Daihatsu Motor Co. 227(tm-bm), 244 — © Mitsuoka Motor Co. 243 — © SsangYong Motor Company 245, 266(tl) — © Kia Motors Corp. 266(bl), 274-276, 292(t) — © BMW AG 267(r) — © BYD Company 268(l), 270(bl) — © Zhejiang Geely Holding Group 268(tr) — © Chery Inc. 268(br) — Qoros Automotive Co. 270(r), 296-297 — © Brilliance China Automotive Holding 269(tl) — Shanghai Automotive Industry Corporation 269(bl) — © Shijiazhuang Shuanghuan Automobile Co. 269(r) — © Shenzen BYD Daimler New Technology Co. 270(tl).

THANKS

For their superb books:

Donald Richie, The Image Factory: Fads & Fashions in Japan; A Tractate on Japanese Aesthetics; A Lateral View: Culture and Style in Contemporary Japan;
Michael A. Cusumano, The Japanese Automobile Industry;
Koichi Shimokawa, The Japanese Automobile Industry;
Wanda James, Driving from Japan;
Vivienne Tam, China Chic.

For their texts, words and deeds:

Giorgetto Giugiaro, Leonardo Fioravanti, Hideo Kodama, Tom Matano, Hideyuki Miyakawa, Tetsu Uemura, Ken Okuyama, Shinichi Ekko, Sharon Kinsella, Dino Dalle Carbonare, Andy Fuchs, Anthia Reckziegel, Michael Bierdumpfl, Lorenza Cappello, Naoki Hayakawa, Wolfram Nickel, Bozo Furkes, Karin Lindel, Rosa Salvia, Sarah Wiesnagrotzki.

Copyright notice

Every picture's source is credited in as precise detail as possible. If anything has been overlooked, the author apologizes and is grateful for any notification. The details could then be updated for future editions.

IMPRINT

Editorial project:
Goodbrands Institute

Goodbrands Institute
Peter-Welter-Platz 5,
50676 Cologne, Germany
Phone: +49-(0)221-348-92-681
Fax: +49-(0)221-348-92-683
e-mail: mail@goodbrands.de

Author: Paolo Tumminelli
Assistant Editor: Christopher Butt
Design: Alice Kaiser

© Paolo Tumminelli, 2014

www.goodbrands.de

Published by:
teNeues Publishing Group

teNeues Verlag GmbH + Co. KG
Am Selder 37, 47906 Kempen,
Germany
Phone: +49-(0)2152-916-0
Fax: +49-(0)2152-916-111
e-mail: books@teneues.de

Press department: Andrea Rehn
Phone: +49-(0)2152-916-202
e-mail: arehn@teneues.de

teNeues Digital Media GmbH
Kohlfurter Straße 41–43,
10999 Berlin, Germany
Phone: +49-(0)30-7007765-0

teNeues Publishing Company
7 West 18th Street, New York,
NY 10011, USA
Phone: +1-212-627-9090
Fax: +1-212-627-9511

teNeues Publishing UK Ltd.
21 Marlowe Court, Lymer Avenue,
London SE19 1LP, UK
Phone: +44-(0)20-8670-7522
Fax: +44-(0)20-8670-7523

teNeues France S.A.R.L.
39, rue des Billets,
18250 Henrichemont, France
Phone: +33-(0)2-4826-9348
Fax: +33-(0)1-7072-3482

www.teneues.com

© 2014 teNeues Verlag
GmbH + Co. KG, Kempen

All rights reserved.
Picture and text rights reserved for
all countries.

No part of this publication may
be reproduced in any manner
whatsoever.

While we strive for utmost precision in every detail, we cannot be
held responsible for any inaccuracies, neither for any subsequent loss
or damage arising.

ISBN 978-3-8327-9538-2

Library of Congress,
Control Number: 2013957673

Bibliographic information published
by the Deutsche Nationalbibliothek.

The Deutsche Nationalbibliothek
lists this publication in the Deutsche
Nationalbibliografie; detailed bibliographic data are available in the
Internet at http://dnb.d-nb.de.

Printed in Italy

FSC
www.fsc.org
MIX
Paper from
responsible sources
FSC® C081623

AUTHOR

Paolo Tumminelli's warm-up lap consisted of architectural studies at Milan before he sped into design, careened into marketing, drove through strategic brand consulting and finally handbrake-skidded to become a Professor at the Faculty of Cultural Sciences at Cologne University of Applied Sciences. In between he was—and still is— a publicist, author, curator, and moderator or, to put it another way: a cultural entertainer. His design column is published weekly in the *Handelsblatt*, Germany's premier economic and financial magazine.

By the same author:

Car Design Europe
ISBN 978-3-8327-9459-0
Car Design America
ISBN 978-3-8327-9596-2

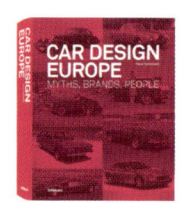

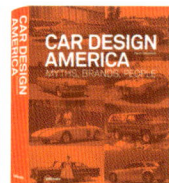